SKIN
in the
GAME:
The Stories
My Tattoos
TELL
Kelly J. Mendenhall

Cindi! -
I'll never be able to
thank you enough.
I love you.
K Mendenhall
(p. 175)

SKIN in the GAME: The Stories My Tattoos TELL

Kelly J. Mendenhall

ISBN
Print Copy: 978-1-7325405-0-7
E-Book: 978-1-7325405-1-4

Author Contact
Kelly J. Mendenhall
hellothere@nerdzillakelly.com
www.nerdzillakelly.com
https://www.anonmomhappyhour.com/

Cover Illustration
Kristen Trawczynski
https://www.facebook.com/MissGogglesIllustration/

Cover & Book Design
Sarah Gzemski
https://www.sgzemski.com/

Photography
Sarah B. Gilliam
https://www.sarahbgilliam.com/

Hair & Makeup
Jill Brooks, The Jill Brooks Beauty Bar
https://www.jillbrooksbeauty.com/

Web Design
Lore de Force
https://www.loredeforce.com

TABLE OF CONTENTS

INTRODUCTION

I got my first tattoo when I was 17 years old. I had *just barely* turned 17. My poor mother never stood a chance. Once I decided I wanted something I went after it relentlessly and my first tattoo was no exception. I remember saying things like, "It could be worse, mom, I could be doing heroin." Another gem was, "I'm not asking for genitalia piercings mom, I could be asking for that!" I also used my stepbrothers to guilt her. "Mom, Thomas and Travis smoke crack, steal cars, and set things on fire. All I want is a tattoo." As I said, I was relentless. Eventually, she broke down and signed the consent form. It was a blanket consent form for, 'Anything except genitalia piercings.'

I had graduated from high school that summer, a year ahead of schedule. It wasn't because I was brilliant or anything, I just had too many credits for the school system to keep me any longer. I thought I was hot shit and that I knew everything. In my defense, I *had* seen and experienced a lot more than most girls my age. Tattoos were the least of my problems and my mother's worries at that time.

I was 16 the day that I met Joey. My best friend Angela and I referred to Joey as 'the hot guy that works at the gas station.' We saw him drawing all the time when we went in there but didn't know he was an artist, let alone a tattoo artist. One day my friend embarrassed the absolute hell out of me, the way all good girlfriends do. She pulled into the parking lot of the gas station, rolled her window down, and shouted, "Hey! My friend thinks you're really hot!" as Joey was walking from the building to his truck. I'm pretty sure I blacked out from embarrassment at that exact moment. I don't remember how the conversation went after that but at some point, we learned that he was headed to the tattoo shop down the street, the shop that his parents owned, where he worked as an apprentice.

I could never have guessed that day (or in the months that followed) that Joey would become such a constant in my life or that I would soon be embarking on the beginning of a lifelong tattoo journey. Over the next ten years, Joey would spend countless hours hunched over my various body parts, placing permanent pictures on my skin. I feel like it's only appropriate that this book begins with him just as my descent into a full-blown tattoos-as-self-expression-and-closure dependence did. I will say, though, that getting at least one tattoo each calendar year keeps me a much more even-tempered and less stabby person. I can purge my body of at least one year's worth of pent-up stress and frustration, sadness, anxiety, and grief in a mere 3-5 hours on a tattoo artist's table.

I'm 36 as I write this and still haven't grown out of wanting tattoos. Much to my mother's chagrin, this is not a phase. I still love almost every piece as much as I did the day I had it done. *Almost.* I doubt any heavily tattooed person doesn't have at least one mild regret, as I surely do. Most of my tattoos are absolute originals, except for my right arm sleeve and a piece of flash I had slapped on my right shoulder blade. I'll tell you more about the sleeve later. But even the pieces I have that were inspired by shop flash or old pieces by Sailor Jerry were customized somehow. My tattoos tell many stories; they tell *my* story.

All of my tattoos represent a person, a place in time, or a significant event in my life. Some of them honor and memorialize dead family members and friends. Some of my tattoos honor people still very much alive who play a significant role in my life. Some of my tattoos have provided me with a great amount of closure and have helped me work through mourning and grief. Some of my tattoos serve as reminders of where I've been or where I'm trying to go.

Every one of my tattoos has a story and I will share most of those stories within these pages. I hope that I've told them well here and that you enjoy reading them.

More than that, I hope that by telling my stories I can help make things just a *little bit* easier for anyone else.

Thanks for indulging me.

CHAPTER ONE

My First Tattoo

Survival, love, and friendship. That's the story my first tattoo tells. When I was 15 years old and a sophomore in high school, I transferred from the school in Chelsea, Michigan, the small town where I lived and was bullied relentlessly, to an alternative high school in Ann Arbor, Michigan called Stone School. Everyone has their idea of what an alternative school is. Some people will see the words 'alternative school' and think of a place only for the worst of the worst kids, where students are totally out of control and have no interest in learning. Some people will think of a school for exceptional or gifted children with a tailored curriculum and teachers that let students call them by their first names. Stone School was something in between.

There were students at Stone who were delinquents, criminals, and ne'er-do-wells and there were also students, like me, who just couldn't hack it in a traditional school environment for whatever reason. My reason was crippling anxiety and the relentless (and often violent) bullying. In addition to the delinquents and me, there were teen moms and dads at Stone who took advantage of the on-site daycare. We also had lazy students who were otherwise harmless but had zero ambition when it came to anything useful. When I think of Stone School I mostly remember freedom from shame. Many of the friendships forged and nurtured in those halls live on today. The story of my first tattoo started there.

Brian with the Curly Dark Hair

Brian and I were in Vietnam War Literature together when we officially met. I was sitting on top of the old radiator along the wall, in front of the windows, waiting for class to start and goofing off with my friends. My friends and I were singing old commercial jingles at the top of our lungs. The Cocoa Wheats song was one of them.

I was wearing blue jeans with holes cut in them strategically so that you could see the spiderwebbed fishnet stockings I was wearing underneath. I donned black, steel-toed combat boots and a t-shirt that read, "Fight Censorship," over a picture of Uncle Sam with a parental advisory sticker over his mouth. My hair was shoulder length and dyed black at the time. I couldn't tell much about him from the unassuming clothes he wore. Solid color t-shirts, blue jeans, hiking boots. That was him pretty much every day. I would later learn that Brian was my polar opposite, into Hip Hop and cyphering[1]. I had seen Brian plenty around the halls and such, but I am certain that we hadn't spoken before this day. The class had started, and our teacher was talking about the book we were reading. The next thing I knew Brian slipped me a note that read: "What's ↑ for tonight?"

I'll never forget that he drew the arrow pointing up like that because my nerdy ass was thinking, what the hell does that mean? It took a moment. I can't even remember what I wrote back, but I can tell you that my heart was in my fucking throat. I didn't know if I was excited or if I was going to puke.

Let me back up really quick.

Did I mention that Brian was *fine as hell*?

I would later learn that Brian was half white, half Chilean. He had dark hair and eyes, perfect teeth, thick lips and a smile that could talk me into just about anything. His skin was like the color of the inside of an almond. Occasionally, he would randomly speak to me in Spanish only to say something as dull as, "Turn off the light."

Swoon, ladies. I know I did. That shit was hot.

I stood zero chance.

I digress.

Brian hands me a note asking me what's up for tonight. My palms started to sweat, and my heart was racing… what did he mean what's up for tonight? Did he not know that I was a total loser with, like, zero plans except homework and that he was *way* out of my

[1] Cyphering in this context means freestyle rapping.

league and what the hell was he doing passing *me* a note talking about what was up for tonight?!

I don't remember what I said, but I know I gave him my number that day. Our first date wasn't long after that. And by date, I mean he drove from Ann Arbor to my house in Chelsea to pick me up and drove me back out to his family's apartment in Ann Arbor where his father and brother were hanging out. My social anxiety was at approximately 75 on a 1-10 scale. I don't really remember anything else about that evening except that I'm pretty sure that was when he gave me a drawing of Spiderman that he'd done… I still have that drawing to this day.

That was it. That was the start of an era. I was helpless and fell head over heels for him in that way that only fifteen-year-old girls can. My first tattoo would forever memorialize this relationship.

Hoodrats

I must not have been the only one who was nervous and hoping to impress, because I clearly remember that on one of our first dates, we were driving down the street and Brian asks me if I like Destiny's Child. Remember that time I said Brian and I were polar opposites? While he was into Hip Hop and R&B, I was the punk rock/skater girl who loved third-wave ska and punk bands like Bad Religion, Propagandhi, and Green Day. (Fuck you, I love Green Day. Still. Judge me.) I look at him like he has something growing out of the side of his face. He proceeds to tell me that his boy, Lynni, is Beyoncé's boyfriend.

"Be-who?"

Clearly, I had a lot to learn.

Brian explained that he and Lynni worked together at Crazy Jim's Blimpy Burger (still the best burger in all of Ann Arbor.) Lynni was born in Detroit, but his family moved down to Texas when he was young. He and Beyoncé lived in Houston and knew one another from a young age. She was his first love and vice versa.

The two were madly in love, but while Lynni was just a regular ass dude like pretty much everyone else he knew, Beyoncé and her girls were in a pop group called – you remember – Destiny's Child. While Destiny's Child was out touring and promoting their album with the insanely hot single 'Say My Name,' Lynni was back up in Michigan refusing just to sit around and wait for his gal to come home.

Not long after Brian and I started dating, he moved out of the apartment where he lived with his father and brother and into a townhouse in a public housing complex in Ann Arbor with Lynni. It wasn't just any complex either – it was North Maple, the neighborhood that at one point had its own mini police station on site. The mini police station was the City's attempt to keep the neighborhood under control. I don't think it was ultimately very effective because by the time I started hanging out there the station was empty.

Since Brian and Lynni had an apartment, I would often stay over with them to get away from my stepbrothers, Thomas and Travis. Staying there meant I could still make it to school without much hassle. While Brian and I were the ones dating, I also became super close with Lynni, so sometimes I'd sleep in Brian's room, but on nights when he was working or out late, I would sleep in Lynni's room, so as not to be alone. Sometimes I stayed for a couple of days at a time, it just depended on how badly things were blowing up at home.

My stepbrothers were into some heavy drugs. They also drank heavily and terrorized my mother and me. My stepbrothers physically assaulted me regularly, frequently threatened to kill my mother and me, and generally terrorized our home and the community at large. They smoked crack in the garage, did heroin in the basement, and drank whatever alcohol they could get their hands on, frequently stolen from their dad's stash. Thomas and Travis were the dictionary definition of evil.

Brian and Lynni really looked out for me. I wasn't allowed to be outside of the townhouse after dark and they rarely left me there alone, *especially* at night. To be frank, white girls were not super welcome in that neighborhood. In fact, there was one night when Brian made me hide in the basement under blankets while he deescalated a situation that was happening outside.

Unbeknownst to us, Lynni had leaned out of the upstairs window and said hello and waved to a couple of girls from the neighborhood. Lynni was all about the southern hospitality, so to him, he was being polite. In the hood, though, that was asking for trouble. I laid under blankets on the basement floor for several minutes listening to Brian talk the situation down outside, explaining that his friend was only being polite and meant no harm. He was able to squash it before it became a serious situation. I was legitimately laying under that blanket thinking, "If those guys outside come inside and down here, what the fuck is going to happen to me?" I never waved at or said hello to anyone in that neighborhood. All things considered, though, it still felt safer than being home with my stepbrothers.

If you're wondering whether I ever met Beyoncé, the answer is no. In fact, she pretty much hated me. Since I stayed there a lot, I answered the phone if the guys were at work, and that annoyed the Hell out of her. She always thought I was trying to hook up with Lynni and steal her man, which is ironic because I was like the one chick hanging out with them that *wasn't* trying to slide under the sheets with Lynni. Although Lynni was a bit of a scoundrel in that he hooked up with other women while Beyoncé was on tour, he did love her. He had their prom photo sitting on his nightstand for all of the years that they were a couple.

My First Tattoo

In addition to Hip Hop and emceeing, Brian was a visual artist. It seemed like he was always drawing something. At one point, he drew a picture of the profile view of a girl; she had her hair pulled back in a simple sloppy bun, one arm was to her side out of sight, and the other was held out in front of her. Levitating above her palm was a flower engulfed in a flame. She had ornate jewelry on and she'd drawn black lines in sort of a swirling pattern around her eye. There was smoke or a mist around her. She reminded me a little of me because of the makeup and the hair. For whatever reason I was enamored with her from the second he drew her.

I was fifteen when Brian drew that character, and I carried her image in my head for two years leading up to begging my mom to let me get my first tattoo. I knew that I wanted my first piece to be that girl.

My friend Joey's dad, the one who owned the tattoo shop, was my tattoo artist for this first piece. He modified the drawing a little bit to incorporate elements that represented him as an artist and what he thought represented my personality well. He put a little stick figure skateboarder on her shirt like a Polo logo, for one thing. The piece was placed on my right thigh. Big Joe was heavy-handed as hell and I *earned* that first tattoo in extra pain alone. I never had him work on me again.

It's been eighteen years since I got that first tattoo. Whenever I look down at it for more than just a second, memories come rushing back and nostalgia overwhelms. I think of Goldie, the kitten that Brian saved from the hood kids who were essentially beating him to death. I think of the time they took me to a club where our friend Dave was spinning for the night and I was served alcoholic drinks and got on a mechanical bull, *wasted*, wearing a skirt. I was 16. I laugh to myself remembering that Beyoncé and the rest of Destiny's Child stopped by North Maple one night after a show in Detroit to visit Lynni. I wasn't there, but from what I heard the hood went *bananas*. I feel like we didn't get fucked with or glared at quite as much after that.

Brian wasn't my first love, but he was close. He introduced me to Blimpy Burgers, liquor mixed with Crystal Light, and rap as poetry. Brian made me fall in love with KRS-One and Common. In comparison to the monsters I was living with at home, Brian was so gentle with me and so protective. He introduced me to one of my most loved and dearest friends and is, honestly, probably the only reason I didn't view all men as dangerous animals.

Spiderman Drawing by Brian with the curly dark hair, 1996, and gifted to me on one of our first dates.

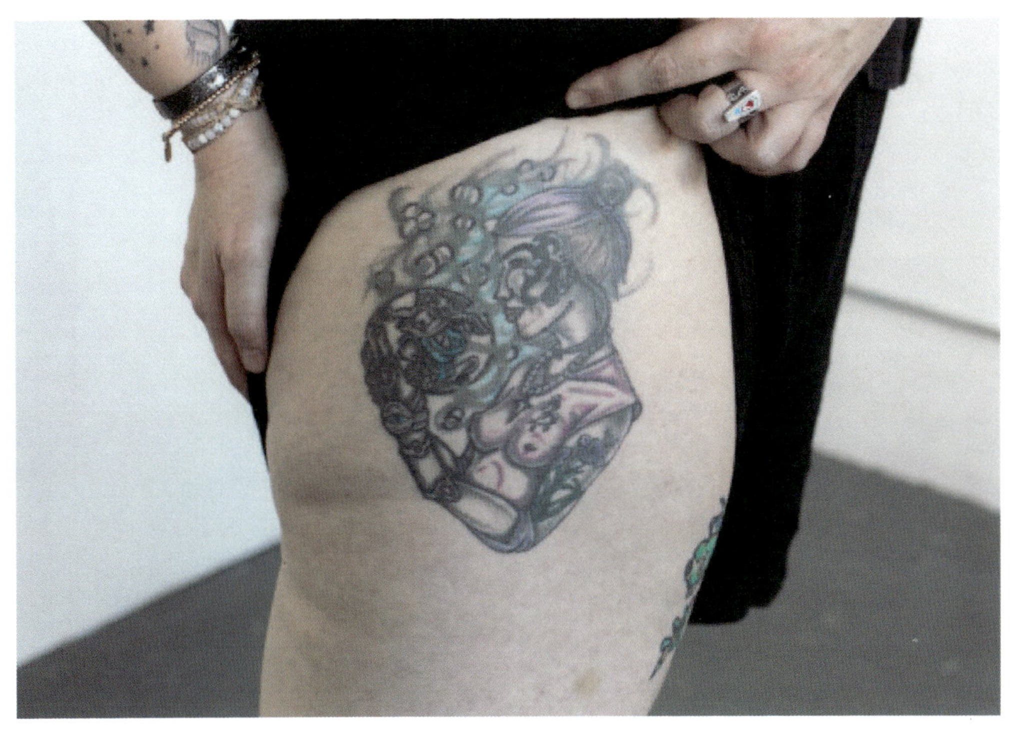

Tattoo done in 1999 at SC Tattooing in Ann Arbor, Michigan. Based on a drawing by Brian. Age at the time of tattoo, 17.

CHAPTER TWO

Honor Thy Father

It was three days after my fourth birthday, August 11, 1986, when my father, Jay Y. Mendenhall passed away from esophageal cancer. Several months prior he had gone to the doctor because he was having difficulty swallowing. X-rays showed a large tumor in my father's esophagus. My mom told me that initially, the surgeons said that it would take 6-8 hours to remove the tumor and get Dad stitched back up. She said that when the surgeon came into the waiting room only three hours later, she knew it would be bad news.

It was.

The cancer had spread throughout his vital organs. They said he only had a few months to live, at most.

My aunt Evie and uncle Jim took on the task of setting my dad up in their home with hospice care. Uncle Jim is my dad's younger brother, and his wife Evie was a nurse. I suppose that dad being in their home for end-of-life care just made the most sense at the time. Evie, Jim, and their three kids lived in Perry, Michigan in a house on a significant bit of property. They lived down the street from where dad's other brother, Herb, lived with his wife Sherry and their kids. This group of the Mendenhalls all lived a couple of hours from where my sisters and I lived with our mom in Davison, Michigan.

It's bizarre, the details that stick in a child's mind about a place and how those memories carry on into adulthood. I remember that on the way to Evie and Jim's we had to drive over a little bridge that went over a small creek and every time we made it to that bridge, I knew that meant that we were almost there. Near the end, I remember sitting on the porch with my dad at Evie and Jim's, playing with toys.

I vaguely remember the day someone took video of my sister Sara and I with our dad, and the person manning the camcorder kept saying, "Tell your daddy how much you love him." Eventually, I turned, the purple Kool-Aid smile I donned on my face visible and held up my hand with all five fingers spread. I said, simply, "Daddy, I love you this much." He replied, softly, "That much? That's a whole lot."

The Big Goodbye

My mother, sisters, and I lived in a single-wide trailer in Davison, Michigan while Dad was set up at aunt Evie and uncle Jim's, living through the business of dying. We had moved out of our farmhouse in Flint, Michigan after dad got sick. My parents had previously been intending on getting a divorce. They sat us all down in that farmhouse one day and told us as much. You wouldn't think I could remember that being only three years old at the time, but I do.

It wasn't long after that, though, that dad went to the doctor and subsequently discovered that cancer was eating him alive. Divorce becomes less of a priority after news like that, I suppose. I remember waking up the day my dad died and walking down the short hallway of the trailer from mine and Sara's shared bedroom into the living room. My mother was hugging Sara over by the couch and they were both crying. I remember feeling confused and uneasy. I remember a part of me not wanting to walk over to my mother and sister, feeling confused and scared by the scene before me. But I did… and my mom pulled me into the embrace and said something along the lines of, "Daddy died in his sleep last night."

I didn't really get it then, but when I say the words in my head now, it feels like someone is punching me in the gut. At the time I felt like I wasn't in on some secret, that they knew something that I didn't know. I thought, "Well, he's been sick… so he died… but he'll get better later and come back." I couldn't wrap my tiny little mind around what was happening.

The next part of the day that I remember is standing on the back porch of aunt Evie and uncle Jim's house, looking in through the sliding glass doors at the room that used to be the dining room but had been turned into my dad's sick room. My dad was still laying there in the hospital bed, and we were all just standing there on the other side of the glass looking in on him. Then someone told my sisters and me to go in and say goodbye.

I *still* didn't grasp what was happening. I was thrown for a loop when I approached the bed and started talking to Daddy, and he failed to respond.

Daddy, wake up.

Wake up, Daddy.

I think it was his face I touched.

I remember that it felt cold.

I turned around and looked at the adults still standing on the other side of the glass.

"Why won't daddy wake up?" I asked.

I remember crying then, but it was less like a sad cry and more like I was crying out of frustration and a little bit of anger because I didn't understand why my dad wasn't responding. My mom told me once that she pretty much lost it when I turned around and asked why he wouldn't wake up. I can't imagine what it would be like for a parent to have to guide their young children through that kind of pain and grief.

My dad didn't want a funeral "with everyone standing around crying about him," so my aunt and uncle planned to have him cremated that same day. One Father's Day my sisters and I had each picked out a rose bush for my dad's garden as gifts. Mom had gotten him a large bench swing made of oak logs. The swing and rose bushes had been transplanted from the farmhouse to aunt Evie and uncle Jim's yard when hospice was initially set up for dad.

The day my father died, my uncle Jim spread his ashes over those rose bushes. While the rest of the details may be fuzzy, I remember with great clarity the moment in which I realized the gravity of the situation. Someone was saying a prayer and it hit me like a ton of bricks…

…Daddy isn't coming back…

That one moment has defined or shaped so many moments in my life to follow.

Two Stone Angels

I was 18 when I traded my friend Joey a watch for a tattoo on my lower back – a tattoo to honor my dad. I loved that damn watch, and I won't lie and say I never missed it. It wasn't anything special, I assure you. I bought it at fucking TJ Maxx. But it was stainless steel, and the band was a metal mesh. It was perfectly me and I loved it. However, I wanted another tattoo, so, there you have it. This was the first tattoo I'd ever had done by Joey.

I was 18 and this was to be my third tattoo. I got two angels that look as though they've been carved in stone like gargoyles.

The text between them reads:

Honor Thy Father
Rest in Peace
1934 - 1986

Unlike my first two tattoos which were very colorful, this one was done in blacks and grays and the look of the angels is somber. The two angels on my back look like young girls. They each hold a single rose.

The tattoo serves to honor and memorialize my dad but I also kind of see it as honoring the four-year-old little girl who had to say goodbye to her daddy far before she was ready and before she could even understand what was happening. That teeny little girl still lives down in my guts somewhere, screaming for someone to comfort her.

This tattoo tells the story of that little girl.

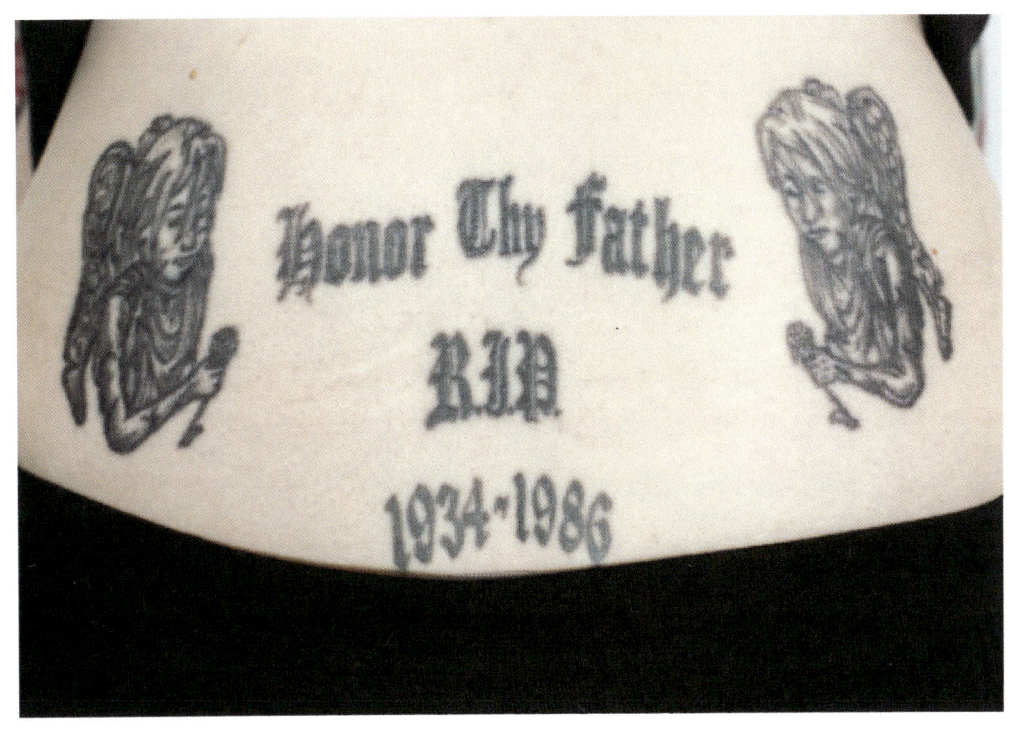

Tattoo completed in the year 2000 by Joey Singleton at SC Tattooing in Ann Arbor, Michigan. Age at the time of tattoo, 18.

CHAPTER THREE

Beautiful Disaster

My First Love

I was 14 the first time I fell in love, with a boy named Rob. I know that many people will read that and roll their eyes and think to themselves something about my being too young to have known what love is. But as I sit here today at age 36 to tell the tale, I still think of him as my first love.

The thing about the nights that change your life is that they're never the nights that you *think* will change your life. The night I met Rob seemed insignificant when it began. My older sister, Sara, 16 at the time, had begrudgingly allowed me to join her and a crew of friends for a night out in Ann Arbor. Ann Arbor is home to the University of Michigan - and its thousands of drunken frat boys and Coeds on a mission to make bad decisions every weekend. It was amidst this crowd and on this night that I first met Dan, Tom, Justin, and Charlie, all close friends of Rob.

After a night of roaming around amidst drunken college students, gutter punks, security guards, and bums, we all returned to Rob's house where no less than seven of us packed into Rob's bedroom for the night to crash.

I didn't know it at the time, but Rob was intended to be set up with our friend April on this particular evening. April was a force within herself. She once dressed as Jesus, complete with the crown of thorns, for Halloween. In 2018 that might not seem *that* shocking but in the early 90s, in a small town where football players got away with everything and an editorial was once published in the town paper about how "no gays live here," it was *incredibly* shocking. April was the freest of free spirits I've ever known and seemingly never spent much time worrying about whether she was weird or what people thought of her.

Rob, on the other hand, was one of the popular kids where he went to high school… *when* he went to high school. He dropped out. He was a snowboarder, part-time pot dealer, and part-time acid dealer, listened to 311 and Sublime almost exclusively (except for the punk rock and ska that his friends forced him to listen to) and could not have been less interested in a girl like April. Or me, for that matter. At least that's what I assumed.

I had a panic attack that night as I was trying to fall asleep. My panic attacks had started when I was in the eighth grade. They were worse when I smoked pot, which I did that night, in an attempt to fit in. I'd taken one too many hits off of a crazy electric bowl. One of the other girls got up to help me calm down, and we went out for a cigarette.

There was a lot of alcohol and pot smoking that happened before we settled in to crash, so everyone was antsy and being packed into the room like sardines wasn't extra comfortable or enticing. When I got back into the room, Dan looks over at me and says, "Rob you should really sit and talk to Kelly. She's a smart girl and you'd really like her."

That was it. That was how it all began.

…And Then He Kissed Me

Rob and I stayed up talking all night; the sun must have been coming up as we fell asleep. I don't remember everything that we talked about, but I remember that the longer I laid there on his bed, barely able to breathe but unable to shut up either, the more I could feel *something* was happening. When he kissed me for the first time, laying there, I thought I might pass out. The whole room was spinning. Even Rob remarked on what felt like the enormity of the situation. It was like an actual electrical shock passed through us. It was one of those nights where, as a teen girl, you question yourself every thirty seconds. "Is this really happening?"

That moment turned into eight months full of moments, good and bad, that defined and shaped my relationship with Rob. I don't know how *your* first sexual experience went, but mine was… eventful. Rob and I were in his basement bedroom, underneath his unwitting parents and little sister, who were watching TV in the living room.

Rob's bed was in sort of a nook within his room. The ceiling was dropped lower and there was recessed lighting. There was a scorpion in a tank with a black light over it, just at the foot of the bed. Dirty clothes were strewn about, everywhere. There were alien posters on the wall if I remember correctly because Rob and the gang were obsessed with 311, which meant a lot of smoking pot and looking for aliens, a lot of dropping the acid that Rob sometimes sold, and a lot of blacklight posters. It was the nineties, don't judge.

So, there we were, two young kids in love, both virgins and hearts pounding out of our chests. We're making out and we know it's totally about to go down. It does, in fact, and all of about sixty-seconds into the experience I'm about to orgasm. Just as the orgasm is about to happen, and mind you I had never had one before so I had no idea they came on so strong, *his mom* knocks on the door.

"Rob? Rob, are you in there?" she beckons.

"What do you want, mom?" he responds.

I assure you that at this point my heart had stopped beating and dropped directly into my stomach. I was also frozen in panic.

"Rob, have you seen the cat?" his mother calls through the door. The family had a long-haired gray cat whose name was, appropriately for more than one reason, Smokey. Rob and I both look over toward the couch and see that the cat is snoozing comfortably and, in my imagination, quite smugly.

"No, mom, the cat's not in here," Rob yells back at his mom, who at this point *has* to be wondering why Rob didn't get up to open the door and speak to her face-to-face.

The entire time they're shouting back and forth, and I still have his penis inside of me, I can't help but think, "Thank fucking God there's a lock on that fucking door."

"Rob, are you sure the cat isn't in there? Can I just come look? None of us have seen him." His mom is pleading now. She has to know, right?!

"Mom! The cat isn't in here!" (Liar, liar, pants on fire.) "I'll come talk to you in a little bit! I'm busy!"

I can't remember exactly how long this exchange went on for, but it felt like 1,000 hours. Eventually, Rob's mom gave up and went back upstairs. We finished our business and he unlocked the door and let the damn cat out of his room. Then, he grabbed a highlighter and wrote the date and our initials on his ceiling, over the bed, so that it would only show up when the black light was on. Romance *abounds*, no?

So, for about eight months or so, I was Rob's girl. What's more than that though, I got to be close friends with all of his friends, the ones I'd met that first night plus Mike. They would stay close friends of mine for years to come. Mike even dated *my* best friend at the time, Mary, which we thought was the coolest shit ever.

The rest of the guys were all really great when Rob and I broke up. Mike was still dating Mary, so he may have been just stuck with me, but the rest of them held no obligation to keep in touch at all. We all did, though, and they brought even more people into my life.

Many nights over the next couple of years were spent around bonfires, under train tracks, or in bedrooms at someone's house trying to be quiet and not wake up parents. There was a lot of underage drinking and, even more pot smoking, but my adolescence would have been much too dull without those guys. My mom probably would have preferred it that way.

Beautiful Disaster

The thing about being a punk-rock-skater-chick and hanging out with all the punk rock kids, the potheads, and the drunks, is that tragedy is bound to strike. I was 15 years old and getting ready for first period, smoking a cigarette outside when my friend Rhiannon walked up to me and asked, "Dude, did you hear about Leone?" For a moment, I thought she meant *Tom* Leone, one of the close friends I gained from my relationship with Rob, and it felt like the wind had been knocked out of my chest. "What do you mean?! What happened to Leone?!" It was actually Tom's older brother, Joe, who'd died. I wasn't as close with Joe as I was Tom, but I *loved* the Leone family (still do) and was devastated for them.

The first time you hear about a friend dying, especially when you're so young, it rocks you in a way that can't be undone. I wasn't a stranger to the concept that life is not ever-lasting, I'd already lost my dad and my maternal grandmother. That's different though. Adults are different.

Rhiannon told me that Joe had been killed in a drunk driving accident the night before.

I fell to my knees.

Rob and I had broken up at this point, and I didn't know what the etiquette was, so it was awkward walking into the funeral. Plus, Tom and Joe come from a huge Italian, Catholic family. So, when I walked into the church alone for the service, I remember looking around at all the slicked-back gray hair and fancy suits. I felt like I was in the middle of a mob movie. Joe was the first of that group, but he wasn't the last, to die young because of alcohol or drugs. Plenty of us almost died in several different ways in years to come.

Charlie died when I was 19. I had just spoken with him a couple of days before and he'd told me about a car accident he'd been in that same week. There had been rumors he'd been hurt or killed but he said he'd actually been fine. We made plans to hang out days later, but I ended up canceling on him. I feel like a dick about that, still, all these years later. We never did hang out again.

I got a phone call from Mike later that week, who said that he had heard Charlie was in a car wreck and had been killed. I was like, "No dude he's fine, I just talked to him the other night. He told me that he'd been in a car accident but it wasn't that bad and he was fine."

Mike came back with, "Are you sure? Can you call his house and ask for him?"

When Charlie's mom answered the phone and I asked for him, she asked if I wanted to speak to Charlie Sr. or Charlie Jr. and I said, "Junior..."

I'll never forget the sound of her voice when she said, "I'm sorry, but..."

There had been a second accident. This time, it really had killed him.

At Charlie's post-funeral reception, we ate Classic Pizza in Dexter and laughed as much as we all could. I saw Rob there, again, just like I had when Joe passed. This time it was twice as awkward because the last contact we'd had, had been when was I was 15 and he and his junkie girlfriend called my house in the middle of the night, high on smack, to tell me that Rob didn't love me anymore and that I needed to move on because this new girl was the love of his life.

I assume that his girlfriend insisted that they place this call after learning that Rob and I had been in contact recently. *He* had called *me* and kept me on the phone for quite some time. He told me all about how he had decided to try heroin and was in love with this other girl, who was also using heroin. He said that if Utopia existed it would be a place where he could love us both and it would be ok.

Mmhm. Right.

The day after receiving this call I went into school a half a day late. I had been crying all night and it showed. My dear friend Bojo, also a heroin addict, asked me what was wrong, and I told him. He listened to me cry about it all day. When Bojo fell off the wagon a short time later, nodding off in English class, I told him that I couldn't watch him die like everyone else. We didn't speak again for another two or three years after that.

On July 4, 2001, Bojo fell off the wagon again and this time he never got back on. He died of a heroin overdose. It was just a few months after Charlie died.

See how the death toll rises so quickly?

There's this song by 311, *Beautiful Disaster*, that makes me cry every time I hear it. It reminds me of all the people that I lost in those few years. All of the people I loved so much that I loved them to death. They lived fast and died young.

On my chest, from shoulder to shoulder, is a tattoo. On the right side when I look down, I see a night sky and glowing moon, clouds floating along. On the left side, a tree with autumn colors in the sky and leaves floating down. In the center of the piece is a flaming sacred star, with a banner that reads, "Beautiful Disaster."

Some of us made it out of all of that alive. I carry the memory of the ones that didn't with me *every. single. day.* I like it that way. I've had people ask me if it makes me sad to think of them every time I look down and see the tattoo. The truth is, the times I spent with all of those guys were some of the best times of my life. I still feel that Rob was my first love (and my first heartbreak) and I still wish that Charlie, Joe, and Bojo had lived. I still wonder or worry about the rest of them often.

Today seems like a good day to burn a bridge or two
The one with old wood creaking that would burn away right on cue
I try to be not like that but some people really suck
Some people need to get the axing chalk it up to bad luck

I know a drugstore cowgirl so afraid of getting bored
She's always running from something so many things ignored
I might do that stuff if it didn't make me feel like shit
I'm on some old reality tip so many trips in it

[Chorus]
Beautiful disaster
Flying' down the street again
I tried to keep up
You wore me out and left me ate up
Now I wish you all the luck
You're a butterfly in the wind without a care
A pretty train crash to me and I can't care
I do I don't whatever

I know a drugstore cowgirl so afraid of getting bored
She's always running from something so many things ignored
I try to be not like this but I thought it'd make a good song
There's nothing to see shows over people just move along

Beautiful Disaster, 311

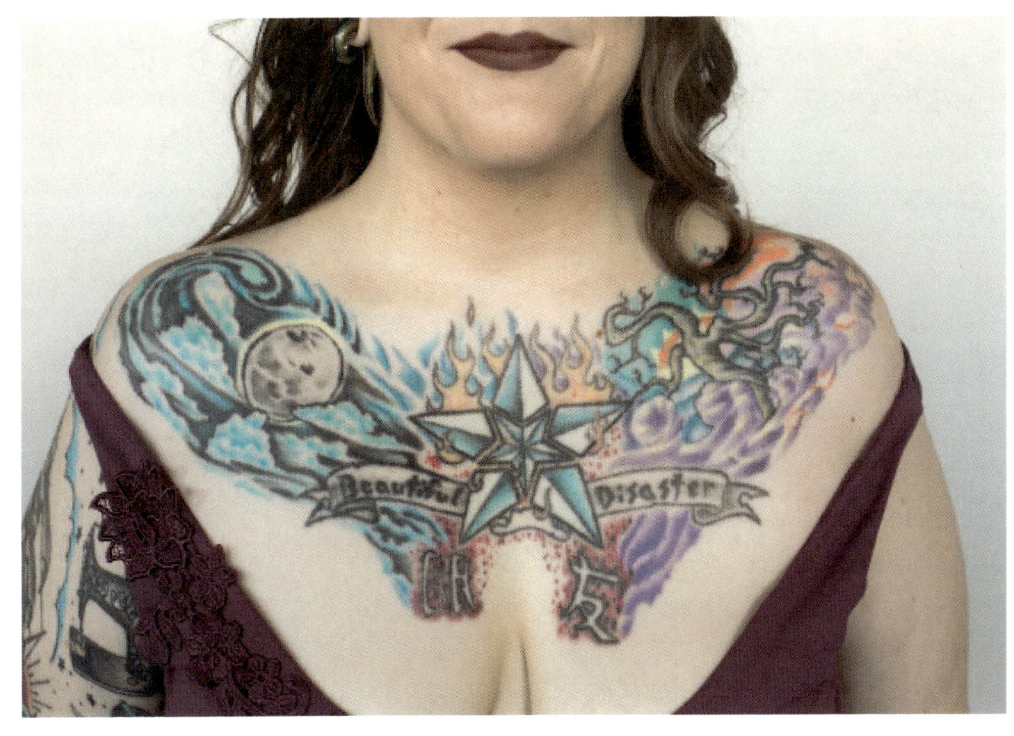

Tattoo completed over a period of years from 2003-2006. Primary artist, Joey Singleton at SC Tattooing in Ann Arbor Michigan. Age at the time of completion, 26.

CHAPTER FOUR

Olive Ewe, or: Greenish-Brown, Female Sheep

Girls are Crazy

I was 11 or 12 years old when I met *her.* It was 6th grade and she was that one friend who is *the worst* possible influence on you. She was a year older than me, but she'd been held back a grade, which meant that she had friends who were a grade ahead of us as well, and she floated between the outcasts and the cool kids. Her ability to fit in anywhere was relatively effortless, whereas I had rampant social anxiety and was an awkward mess. I don't remember how we became friends, I just know that around 7th or 8th grade she started showing up in my photos and in my memories.

One of my first memories of her is also the one that sticks out in my head as the biggest red flag. I should have seen her special brand of crazy coming from a mile away. It was the night she showed up at my house unannounced and intoxicated…when I was *twelve.* She showed up at my house with some other middle-school-aged girl and a carload of guys accompanied them. The guys were in their twenties and I am pretty sure they had all been drinking and/or were high when they arrived.

Angela came to the door unannounced, accompanied by this girl I didn't know, maniacally jazzed up about something. I immediately felt uneasy and decided this was best kept out of earshot of my mother and pushed the girls out onto the front stoop. How I kept the ruckus down enough for my mom not to venture outside and ask, "What the hell is going on?!" I will never know. All I can remember is that, as quickly as they showed up and I encountered this weird blur that was Angela, the car suddenly sped off with all of them in it. And that was that. This encounter maybe lasted twenty minutes. I didn't even know what to think.

This was only the beginning of the weird shit that would happen over the many years of friendship with Angela. I remember being in 8th grade and hanging out at Angela's house with a mutual friend when Angela started acting *really* strange. She began talking about how her dad was going to beat her when he got home from work because we'd asked her mom for a cigarette. She told us over and over again that he was going to beat her ass when he got home. Then she just wandered out into the field between her house and the neighbors and disappeared for about a half an hour. When she came back she was barefoot and disheveled and told us that she had been hearing voices. Part of me knew she had to be completely full of shit and part of me was scared shitless. Who was this girl?!

For what it's worth, I spent probably entire months' worth of overnights at her house. Throughout our years of friendship, I never once saw her dad beat her or even raise his voice. This was in spite of our propensity for showing up to the house with male counterparts, drunk, to swim in the family pool late at night. Often, we emerged from her basement bedroom with obvious hangovers. Her dad was never more than gruff, skeptical, and tired of our shit. I still carry a great deal of affection for her parents, as they tolerated and loved me throughout the years and in spite of our many shenanigans.

Like Sand Through the Hourglass

Being friends with Angela was like flirting with danger on a daily basis, and not always in the most fun ways. She was a train wreck of human emotion. I am almost certain now she had/has an undiagnosed mental illness. Angela was always the girl who loved to test boundaries. She would walk up to a guy she was dating and for no apparent reason punch him dead in the face. She would lie and cheat her way through every relationship she found herself in and seemed to get off on manipulating and ruining men.

I saw her drive two men crazy, watched her slowly deteriorate their mental fortitude and well-being through constant mind games and psychological abuse. Observing Angela's romantic relationships was like watching a surrealist soap opera with the volume so loud it's almost too painful to watch.

At the same time, she was a lot of fun to hang out with. She was rowdy as shit, always had your back in a fight, loved a good mosh pit, always had cigarettes and knew where to find booze, and she made staying up until 4:00 AM seem entirely reasonable. Usually, you were laughing so hard you didn't notice time passing anyway. All of these skills became especially useful to me after high school.

I was only sixteen when I graduated from Stone School and in the throes of PTSD that no one had diagnosed yet. Angela dropped out of high school that year or the year before, so we had a whole lot of partying and mischief to dive into. And did we ever dive right in...

The Meth Heads

The summer after I graduated from high school Angela and I worked at Pizza Hut with two guys who were also best friends. They were *also* meth heads. We met up with them one night to party.

We were in the middle of nowhere, in Stockbridge, Michigan. When we were trying to find the house that one of the guys lived in, he said to look for the white house with a pickup in the driveway. Every house on that road was white... with a pickup truck in the driveway. I remember joking that if anything happened to us we'd have no way to tell anyone where we were or how to find us. Looking back, I can't help but think, "How the hell am I still alive?" But this was normal for us. Or at least not *that* bad, comparatively.

Angela and I consumed three bottles of cheap wine that night, each. We each hooked up with our respective meth head in the living room of the house. Angela and her guy on the couch, myself and my guy on the floor. The shame and disgust I felt on the drive home the next morning, just as the sun was rising, was palpable. We were both hungover and probably still a little bit drunk. We also had to be to work in a matter of just a few hours. We swore never to speak of that night again and I promised myself I would never be *that* wasted and *that* irresponsible with my body again.

The Suicide Machines

Later that same summer we went to see the Suicide Machines (a Detroit band) outdoors in some killer summer heat. It was a huge summer radio festival put on by 89X. We had one of the meth heads with us, and he hadn't had a fix for several hours. He was more than a little in need of a stiff drink by the time we arrived because, as it turns out, he was also a drunk. The guy Angela was dating at the time locked my keys in the car as we descended upon the park to figure out where we were going. We were soon faced with a choice: Smash out a window to get the booze from the back of the car, or let the alcoholic meth head go into full-blown withdrawal in the middle of a rock concert, crawling with park security.

I was barely 17 and had no clue whom I would call or how I would call them to help us, so I let him smash the window. That window was never fixed; the following winter was *cold.*

The Ex-Boyfriend

Right on the edge of summer and fall that year, Angela's ex-boyfriend, the first guy I saw her drive crazy, showed up at Pizza Hut and was waiting for her when we walked out into the parking lot. I hung back while they argued in the parking lot and could hear him insisting that she let him get in her car and ride back home with her. She and I were supposed to be on our way to her house where several of our coworkers were planning to meet up to get drunk and play in the pool.

Angela told me to go ahead and get in my car and follow her home. My gut told me that something terrible was about to happen. I didn't anticipate that it would include me following her car, speeding around 100mph in the dark for 15 miles from Ann Arbor to Chelsea.

We didn't have cell phones back then, so there was so no way to call her and ask her why her car was swerving, stopped abruptly, and then took off again like a bat out of hell down the road. I just followed as closely as possible, knowing it must have been some kind of an emergency.

Eventually, she screeched into the parking lot of Chelsea Hospital, parked in front of the Emergency Room, and ran from the driver's side to the passenger side door of the car. It turned out that the ex-boyfriend had tried to take the wheel of the car and drive them both off the road. When he wasn't able to overpower her to get control of the vehicle, he slit his wrist.

Blood was everywhere. This was the same ex-boyfriend who assaulted me and tore the rotator cuff in my shoulder one night when I got in the middle of their argument and tried to persuade her to stop fighting with him. The most surprising thing about that was that he and I had been nearly inseparable, like siblings, just a couple of years before they started dating.

We all have one crazy friend, don't we?

It was never a secret that my mom couldn't stand Angela. Thankfully, she never knew the extent of all of the shit that we got into, but it doesn't take much maternal instinct to know when your kids are up to no good. This is especially true when that something regularly involves drugs and/or alcohol. I never did more than smoke pot when I was in high school, and even that was short-lived. However, my friends were up to plenty else and my mom knew it. I was pretty honest with her about that type of thing, surprisingly.

Looking back now, I am convinced that my mom's trust in me played a big part in my *not* going down the same path that many of my friends did. The standing rule in our house was that if myself or my sister were at a party and found ourselves with no sober ride, we could call home and my mom would come and get us, no questions asked, and we wouldn't be in trouble. I had to do it at least two or three times and every time I expected that she would show up raging, red-faced, and yelling at me. She kept her word, though, I never got in trouble.

In spite of my mother's many objections, I continued to hang out with Angela, even after I started to get my life together, while she remained trapped in the same spiral of havoc she'd been in since the day I met her.

We all have a crazy friend when we're young, don't we? Ladies, you know the one I mean. The friend who would follow you into the front lines of battle one minute and the next won't even look at you. You can go weeks or months without speaking to one another because she gets pissed off about something you said or didn't say and she can hold a grudge like nothing you've ever seen before.

When I was 18, Angela stopped speaking to me. She was pregnant with her first-born son and was about to marry his father. He would be the second man I saw her drive to the edge of sanity. I had unwittingly introduced the two, as he was also one of my closest friends. I met him when I was in high school at Stone School. He was similarly crazy, but not *quite* on her level. For those years when he was tangled up in her, they were quite the matched set.

One night, when I was 18, I was hanging out at a Steak 'N Shake in Ypsilanti, Michigan, with some friends. Among these friends included a guy Angela had hooked up with behind her boyfriend's back, right before she got pregnant. I can't remember how he found out, but he showed up a short while later with a knife.

I called Angela's house to tell her. To try to get her to talk to him and help him calm down, but she wouldn't get on the phone. So, I told her mom what had happened instead, hoping she would get Angela to talk some sense back into her boyfriend. Angela was pissed off that I said anything to her mom, and it would be years before I heard from her again.

Guess Who's Back?

Fast forward four years. I was in my college dorm pulling an all-nighter writing a paper when I heard from Angela out of the blue on Myspace. I remember *actually* holding my breath when the message came up as I tried to think of a way to respond. Was this a setup? I mean, you never knew with her. Within a few minutes, we were talking and catching up as though no time had passed at all. She told me that she and her husband (the boyfriend with the knife) now had two boys, who were two-years and one-year-old, both born in August, their birthdays only a few days after mine.

Angela and the kids were in Georgia while her husband was serving in the Army. They were, she said, separated because he had cheated on her while he was deployed overseas. Angela moved back to Michigan not long after we spoke. She and the boys moved into her parents' house.

Angela and the boys were planning to live there for an indeterminate amount of time. She said she planned to go to school because she wanted to be a nurse. She loved blood and gore - she literally used to laugh while she was getting tattoos because she enjoyed the pain. Unfortunately, nursing school lasted for about one semester.

From about 2005-2008, I was deeply entangled in the lives of Angela and her two boys. So much happened in those years that it's hard to keep track. I feel like I lived five lifetimes in that handful of years. I quickly became known and accepted as Aunt Kelly and the boys became the light of my life. For years while their father was on active duty overseas, I helped raise them.

I was their nanny for the one summer their mom attempted to attend college. I was at every birthday and holiday. I even helped potty-train the youngest brother. I also helped re-potty-train the older brother after their dad was deployed for his second tour in Iraq and he refused to use the "big boy potty until daddy came home safe." I remember teaching the youngest his first words and helping him practice his pronunciation. His first word was "happy." I delighted in the way he said it, "**HAP**-pee" with a pause in the middle of the word for emphasis.

In 2005 I had moved into a house with my boyfriend about ten miles from where Angela lived. I was with her and the boys pretty much every day. In October 2006, when I broke up with the boyfriend and had no place of my own I decided to rent an apartment closer to campus, about 40 miles from where we were all living at the time.

Angela and the boys rented an apartment across the way from me, in the same complex, just a month or so later. We became this little weird atypical family and I loved being able to help with the boys so much. We had dinner together most nights and I helped get the boys to and from preschool. In spite of how busy everything was, life was pretty chill.

Things got significantly less chill in December 2006 when I found out that my fourteen-year-old niece and oldest sister were having such a hard time getting along that they were getting into fist fights and the police were being called for domestic disputes. I had no idea what I was signing up for when I told my sister to send my niece to live with me. She became part of our little family too, for a time, but it wasn't long before everything imploded.

Not so HAP-pee

Over the next six or eight months, I took on a teenager who turned out to be using a lot of drugs, having a lot of sex, and doing a lot of pathological lying. It was like watching my younger self through the eyes of an adult who made it to the other side, but I was powerless to stop the inevitable train wreck. My niece wasn't having it. She rebelled against anything and everything I tried to do for her.

In January 2007, I lost two of my best friends in the same week — Mark died in combat and Jeff died from complications with pneumonia he didn't know he had. In February, I traveled abroad for the first time, attending a study abroad program in London with my friend Bridget. (It was also my first time flying, and I was scared *out of my mind,* to put it mildly. It took *a lot* of drugs to get me on that plane.) Then, I graduated from college that April. The job I'd had since 2005 was a campus job, so as soon as I graduated from college the job was gone too.

It didn't take long before I was tapped on resources. I mean, beyond drained. I was living off of credit cards to support my niece and keep us housed, clothed, and fed. I was job hunting to no avail and going through a bit of a mental collapse because of everything that had happened in such a short amount of time — losing Mark and Jeff, graduating, losing my job, and dealing with serious family drama. It was all too much.

I had no idea what to do or how to do it. But when I called my sister to tell her that I couldn't support my niece anymore, she told me that she wouldn't take her home, either. Meanwhile, Angela's behavior was becoming more and more erratic, and now so was my niece's.

I'd already figured out by this point that my niece and her friends were much more out of control than I'd ever dreamt of being at her age. They were stealing cars and joyriding all day instead of going to school, dropping acid, and all sorts of other terrible things. I only figured this all out after installing keystroke tracking software on every computer she had access to.

Reading through all of the emails and social media messages revealed that my niece had her friends convinced that she had cancer. She was also reasonably believable when she described how I was abusing her. She had even persuaded them at one point that she was out of my apartment and homeless. This was, of course, all news to me. Even after all of this, my sister refused to intervene. So, Angela suggested that my niece could live with her.

My sister agreed to this arrangement, much to my dismay, and all I could do was sit back and watch as everything devolved into a crazy white trash soap opera. At this point, I slipped into a full-on psychological breakdown; the kind where you drink a lot and listen to Waylon Jennings and Tim Barry, staying up until 6:00 AM drinking, singing, and crying. I called it my quarter-life crisis.

It was just all too much. The heartache was so deep I couldn't hold myself up under the weight of it anymore. I'd lost two beautiful, dear friends, all respect for my oldest sister (who up to this point had been my best friend), and lost my relationship with my niece, whom I'd helped raise because she had become teenage hellspawn. I also had zero fucking clues about what I was doing with my life.

The breakdown lasted for several weeks before my best-friend-who-was-more-like-a-brother told me that if I didn't snap out of it he was going to call my mom. I got a tattoo to commemorate the experience, it's an Exploding Dog cartoon (Google it.) A stick figure is standing over one star, which has fallen to the ground and does not look well, where a happy-looking star floats above and is looking down on the scene. The text to the side says, "Please get up."

I got up.

Begrudgingly, and with much less chutzpah than I'd previously had. But I got up.

Life resumed its weird brand of ordinary and I dove back into family life with Angela and the boys, along with my niece.

Don't ever think it can't get worse

What I know now is that Angela was highly addicted to pain pills and was selling them. She was also openly using them in front of my niece and her two sons. I learned many years later that she even started supplying my niece with drugs, using them as a bribe for my niece to stay up with her and clean the house. I had a feeling back then that *something* was going on, and tried calling my sister to convince her that it wasn't safe for my niece to live with Angela anymore.

The warnings fell on deaf ears. My sister, of course, confronted Angela with the things I'd told her and Angela convinced her that I was crazy and that everything at her house was just fine. It was utterly surreal to live through.

Meanwhile, Angela's kids were still my world. Some days I think they were the only thing that kept me going. At some point, the boys became enthralled with the cartoon movie Robots and began speaking in Robot-Speak. They would say, "I love you, Aunt Kelly. Beep beep," or "I'm a robot, beep beep." They would act like robots with stiff joints and walk around the apartment bumping into things or falling over and pretending their batteries had run out. I played along and called them my little robots.

About this time, I started dating a tattoo artist named Brandon. He was a mediocre tattoo artist and a subpar human being. I was in such a depressed and defeated state of mind that I was the perfect girl for a raging alcoholic narcissist. He was about my fourth raging alcoholic narcissist romantic partner at this point in my life.

Brandon was really good at playing the victim and pretending like he really, really was trying to get himself together – it was just that everyone was against him and wanted him to fail. My financial situation went from bad to worse as Brandon moved into my place. He hoarded all of his earnings from tattooing and proceeded to suck the life out of me physically and emotionally. Looking back, I realize that he and Angela were just male and female counterparts and they were both sucking me dry. No surprise, then, that they would stay in touch as friends long after I kicked both of them out of my life.

Before I worked up the courage to kick Brandon out of my apartment he put three tattoos on me, one for Angela and two for the boys. When Angela and I had been in high school we used to say "Olive ewe," or, "greenish-brown female sheep," instead of I love you. We'd heard it on a Lifetime movie. So, to commemorate our friendship I got an olive ewe. It looks a lot like the Serta sheep, but she's colored like an olive.

I got two robots for the boys; one is dragging his heart behind him and the other is floating in the clouds, carried away by the heart balloon tied around his waist. I used to tell the boys that the flat hearted, sad robot was what I looked like before they came into my life and the happily floating balloon-heart robot was what my life looked like with them in it.

Angela's husband would come and go whenever he had leave and it was always really hard to tell what was actually going on between them. She would swear that they were divorced and she wanted nothing to do with him, but whenever he was in town he still acted romantically interested.

Sometime in 2007, he came home for good, stationed back in Georgia. Angela and the boys moved there to be with him, taking my niece along as well. Over the next year, Angela would travel back and forth to Michigan a handful of times. Each time, her behavior would be more erratic. Her husband would try and tell me that she was doing heavy drugs, specifically cocaine, and needed help. For whatever reason, I refused to believe it.

What I didn't know then is that she was using cocaine quite heavily, in addition to the pain pills, and dropping acid whenever her husband was away, according to what my niece told me years later. To add insult to injury, she and her friends were providing the drugs to my niece, who was just 16.

Finally, enough is enough

In 2008, Angela drove up to Michigan with my niece and the boys the week that my middle sister got married. My niece and I attended the wedding while Angela went on a bender. My niece finally went back home with my oldest sister, to Florida, after the wedding. Over the next week, Angela kept trying to withdraw cash from my niece's checking account where her social security check was deposited each month.

It wasn't long after the wedding when Angela's parents would be away on a cruise; I would be in El Salvador for a Study Abroad program (I had just started graduate school in May 2008) and Angela would be shacked up in her parents' home on a Heroin bender. She and the junkie guy who was with her pawned all her mother's jewelry and stole all the cash her dad had at the house. The boys were with her the whole time.

When I came back from El Salvador two weeks later, I returned to dozens of panicked voicemails from Angela, screaming at me that she was pregnant again and needed an abortion. She was furious, how could I do this to her and refuse to answer my phone?

I called her back and reminded her that I'd been in Central America. Next thing I know, she shows up at my apartment with both boys.

They looked like they'd been through Hell. They were crying, saying that they were hungry. It looked like they hadn't had a bath in days. I asked her when the boys had last eaten, she responded with a surprising amount of apathy, "I don't know!" At one point during her visit, Angela turned and snapped at her oldest son, "Yeah… well, next time your dad calls tell him you're fucking hungry." At that moment I knew that her husband had been right all along, and I was a fool.

I didn't have much food in my apartment, but I cooked up all of the miscellaneous odds and ends I could find and fed them. It was a small buffet of frozen chicken tenders, French fries, and other things. When Angela left with the boys, she told me that they were going to a house that I was pretty sure was rampant with junkies and neer-do-wells. I immediately called her husband.

I told him he needed to get to Michigan ASAP because the boys were not safe with Angela. I said I was sorry that I hadn't listened, that I had argued with him. It was painfully apparent that something was *very* wrong.

Weeks later, Angela's parents and husband had agreed on a plan. Angela was pretending to have a job at a bar. Hell, maybe she actually did work there, I don't know. The idea was to wait for a night when she said she would be working. After Angela left, her parents called her husband, who called me. I drove my car to Angela's house where I met her husband. We loaded the kids and as many of their belongings as we could into his SUV. I'll never forget the look on her family's faces. Her parents and oldest sister looked not only devastated but terrified.

Her dad turned to me and said, "I always thought it would be you. I figured with all the crazy hair, shit hanging out of your face and the tattoos, that you'd be the one who was on drugs." There was a small part of me that just for a moment wished that it was me so that I didn't have to see the pain in his eyes as he watched his grandsons loaded into a car, not knowing when he might see them again.

The boys rode with their dad and I followed behind. We drove to Ann Arbor and stopped again, at Joey's parents' tattoo shop, so that I could say goodbye one more time. Then their dad took them home to Georgia.

That was the last time I saw them.
I walked inside to tattoo the pain away.
I haven't spoken to Angela since.

Olive Ewe tattoo done by toxic ex-boyfriend in a friend's apartment in 2008, when I was aged 26.

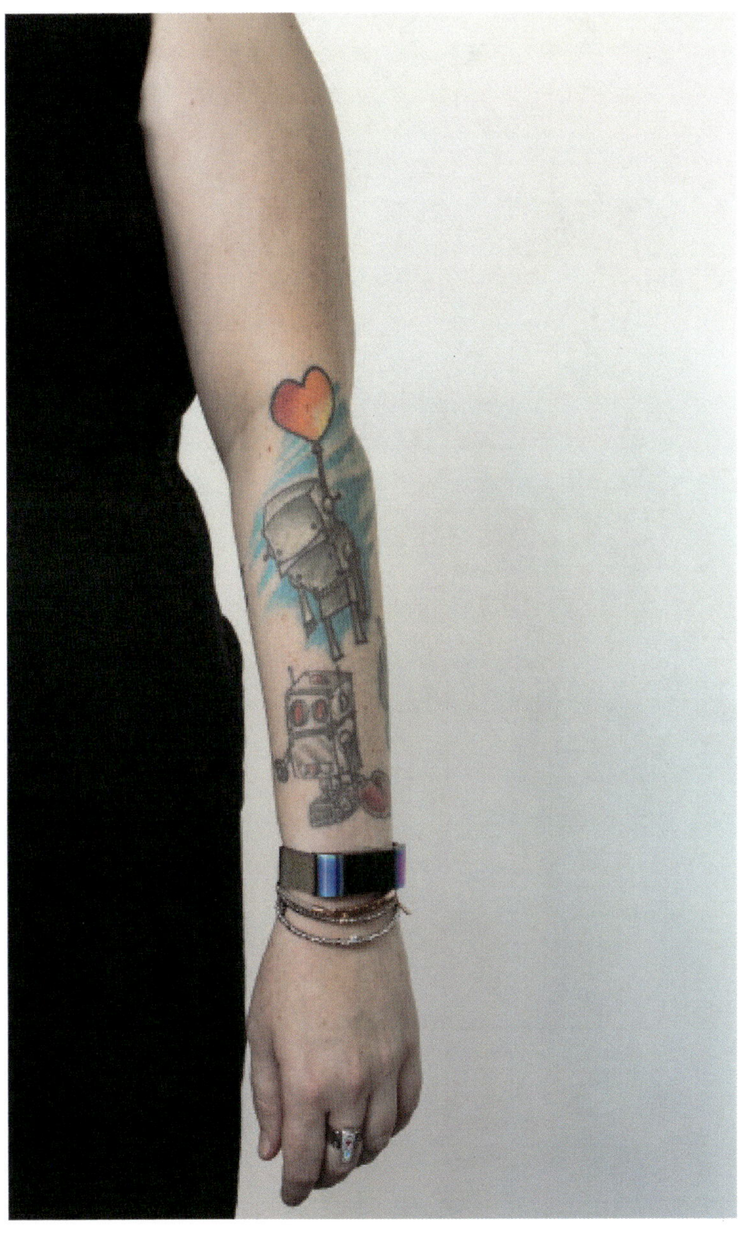

Robot with the sad heart done by toxic ex-boyfriend's boss at Lost & Found Tattoo Company in Ypsilanti, Michigan, 2008. Robot with the happy heart started by toxic ex-boyfriend, corrected and completed in 2009 by Larry Shelby of Empire Tattoo Company in Redford, Michigan, when I was 29.

Fallen star star and stick figure that states, 'Please get up.' This tattoo was originally a drawing on www.explodingdog.com, artist Sam Brown

CHAPTER FIVE

The Midnight Train

See the hills from afar standing on my beat up car
The sun went down and the night fills the sky
Now I feel like me once again as the train comes rolling in
Smoked my boredom gone, slapped my brains up so high
Give me something to do to kill some time
Take me to that place that I call home
Take away the strains of being lonely
Take me to the tracks at Christie Road

- Green Day, "Christie Road"

Flint, Michigan

I was born and spent my younger, formative years in Flint, Michigan. Our stepdad, Ken, moved in around the same time dad passed. My parents were already splitting up when we found out my dad had cancer. Although we moved to Davison for a few years throughout dad's illness, we landed back in Flint when I was five or six. It was just before a birthday for me.

Flint is not an easy place to grow up.

Flint was scary. We couldn't wear the Starter jackets we got for Christmas when I was in the sixth grade because kids were getting shot and robbed for them way too often. There was also the issue of accidentally wearing gang colors in the wrong territory, because the jackets were brightly colored to match the sports teams represented.

Nike shoes were another thing that kids would get shot and robbed for. A friend of mine missed school once in the fourth grade because a bullet grazed her head when she was on her way to school with her mother and sister. My friend and her family lived in the North End of Flint, which has always been the worst part of town, for as long as I can remember. There was a drive-by shooting that morning, and their family just happened to get caught in the cross-fire.

When I was 11years old, my mother and stepfather decided to move my sister Sara and me out of Flint once and for all. Amber was already on her own by then, in college and with a child of her own. My parents decided to leave for the same reasons everyone else wanted to leave, I suppose — the violence, the poor jobs, and shitty schools, and for the change of scenery and a fresh start.

My parents were right to have concerns about us living out the rest of our young lives in Flint — it didn't have much of a future to offer us. We moved to a small town about 60 miles south of Flint called Chelsea. It was one of many towns that were conveniently located just far enough away from Detroit, for white people who wanted to work in the city but not live there. Its only claim to fame is that this is where Jiffy Mix (yes, the corn muffin mix) is made.

Chelsea offered no diversity, no tolerance, and no room for us. We were hated in part because we were the new kids in town and in part because, where we came from, there were black people. Moreover, we were friends with them. Imagine, the horror! It was an absolute shitshow living in Chelsea and I was bullied from about the very moment I arrived until the moment I left Chelsea schools and switched to Stone High School in Ann Arbor in 10th grade.

My Vietnam

After a few years in Chelsea, when I was around 12, my mom and stepdad split up. I was 14 when my mother became engaged to my second stepfather, Mark, or John Doe Dad No. 2, as I came to call him. (I was a little damaged by my mom's split with my first step-dad.) After the engagement, our families were blended into one dreadfully dysfunctional household consisting of myself, my mom and stepdad, my older sister Sara, and my two stepbrothers.

My stepbrothers, who were twins, were almost exactly one year older than I was. They were the closest thing to pure evil I have ever encountered. Our parents hadn't even married yet when one of them strangled me until I was nearly unconscious, a friend intervening and pulling him off from on top of me just in time.

I was 15 when that same twin held a butcher knife to my throat and, again, a friend intervened. You see, my stepbrother had been harassing my best friend Mary and when I told him to leave her alone he punched me in the tit. I was wearing a 1" spiked bracelet and brought it straight down into his arm. He went upstairs and grabbed a butcher knife and cornered me in the basement where I was sitting on the couch. My friend Chris told my stepbrother that he could go ahead and slit my throat with that knife, but that he was confident he could get his gun and shoot him dead faster than the speed at which my stepbrother could get away. I still believe this is the only reason why he didn't actually do it. This is perhaps the greatest irony of my life — my mom moved us out of Flint to get us away from the crime and violence. We ended up in a quiet, shithole town where all the violence and crime lived under the same roof as us.

In the approximately three years that we all lived in the same household, I was, along with my mother, subjected to regular verbal threats, physical violence, and drug-addled rages perpetrated by the twins. They regularly described to my mother how they were going to kill her. There were times when I stepped between her and them to spare her of whatever they were hurling at her and to take it onto myself.

One summer the police were at our house dozens of times in one month. Our home became so well known that when I later got a job at a gas station in Ann Arbor and got to know some of the officers and firefighters who came in as regular customers, they knew where I lived just by hearing my name, or the name of my stepbrothers. The Scio Township Fire Chief really came to look out for me in the time I spent working at that gas station.

When I worked up the courage to tell my mom that one of the twins was regularly grabbing my breasts and calling me "sweet tits" she confronted their father and he basically responded with 'boys will be boys.' I did not dare to tell her about the time that I was coerced into performing oral sex on one of their friends.

In front of them.

On the floor of our garage.

I didn't finally tell her until I was in my early twenties.

The twins shot heroin, smoked crack, and drank heavily in and around our home, committing a laundry-list of crimes while under the influence. Every time they were arrested, I would hope that that would be the time they stayed in jail and we would be safe for a while. Unfortunately, their father had a decent income and bailed them out repeatedly (and pretty much immediately). I will never forget the night when he said, with pure hatred and vitriol hurled at my mother, that his sons were innocent pawns in a sick and twisted game that she and her daughter were playing. That man was the King of Denial Island.

Whatever childlike innocence I clung to after leaving Flint was annihilated while living with the twins and Mark. I found out recently, at the age of 35, that the police chief in Chelsea (came to our house one day to talk with my mom. He told her that it wasn't a habit of his to tell other people what to do with their lives, but that "those boys were going to kill someone eventually" and that he didn't want it to be her or her girls. Thank God he decided to stick his nose in our business and have that talk with my mom that day. It seems to have impacted her decision to get the hell out of there when she did.

The Midnight Train

During the years with my stepbrothers, my friends became my salvation — they were my real family. Back then I didn't just hate going home — most nights I was *afraid* to. So, I'd take any opportunity I could to stay out as late as possible. These circumstances are why I spent such a significant amount of time at Brian and Lynni's apartment in high school.

The ritual of watching the midnight train with my group of deeply-bonded friends started and ended the summer I turned 15. Those summer nights on the shores of the Huron River were always ones to remember. There were few life-changing moments, but to me that whole summer was life-changing. My friends and I hung out on the banks of the river and waited every night for our dreams to screech by on the rails of the train tracks.

Our tradition was to watch the midnight train and dream

about where it might take us and what we would do once it got us there. This was the kind of whimsical romanticism I believe one only gets to enjoy during adolescence. After the train passed, usually sometime after midnight, we would go to the Fleetwood Diner, in downtown Ann Arbor, for chili-cheese fries and coffee. We would talk for what seemed like forever about whatever we were dreaming or carrying in hearts.

This core group that hung out so frequently that summer included: Erin and her sister Jenny, Rhiannon and Chris (the group's power couple), Brian (a different Brian, not my boyfriend but more like a brother), and myself. Most of us had something we were running away from or something new we wanted to see or do. Rhiannon always talked about California. By this time, I was dreaming of being a famous writer in New York City. The thirst for adventure was quenched for us all just a little, every night when the midnight train came in.

The environment around the river is beautiful; Huron River Drive is a windy road canopied by trees and surrounded by wooded areas, parks, and nature reserves. It was generally quiet and peaceful on the part of the river where we used to sit up under the trestles so that passersby wouldn't detect us. The only noise came from the train and us.

Rhiannon was famous for asking the most random questions. Something like, "Kelly, would you still love me if my eyes were orange?" The way that Rhiannon always posed these types of questions, always if X is Y then will you still love me, it was like she was afraid that at any moment she would blink and we would all disappear. I would regularly respond with, "I'll always love you, Nannon, even if all the stars fall from the sky." She would smile and take that as good enough assurance.

Chris was wild, a total redneck deeply entrenched in a crew full of city kids. He drove his Mustang like he was Mario Andretti and I am still amazed we never had any wrecks if I'm being perfectly honest. When I think of him that summer, I can picture him, stoned on pot, walking on the rails in a one-man balancing act. He always called us fuckers, like that was our collective name. "I don't know, fuckers, what does it look like I'm doing? Hehehe…" That's how I hear him in my head thinking back.

Chris must have been 17 or 18 back then because he was older than us and wasn't ever in school at the same time we were. Chris was a hick and a pig, but you had to love the guy, if for no other reason than because he could always make you laugh. He was a goofball, but he was serious about his friendships. Chris looked out for everyone, especially me, and is the same friend who persuaded my stepbrother not to slit my throat.

Brian and Chris were like brothers to one another, absolute best friends. Brian was a criminal, honestly, not unlike a lot of my friends back then. You can call it a cliché if you want, but the thing about it is, you hang out with the hardest people possible when you're living inside a live explosive, ready to be detonated at any moment.

I hung out with criminals and thugs because they took care of me. And there was this strange code of conduct among them, too, as though I wasn't to be touched by the dumbass shit they were up to. I remember more than once when members of the crew would hug me, tell me they loved me, and say goodbye out of nowhere. That was my cue that trouble was about to pop off and I best get as far away from it as possible.

Erin was a total spaz and a had a gluttonous appetite for attention. She often came off as faking or exaggerating anxiety attacks and bad drug trips just so that everyone would fawn over her. Most of the time we all played into it because, no matter how you looked at it, something was eating that girl up inside. Even if it was only herself. Rhiannon was Erin's best friend and like a sister to me, but she was also a bit of a spaz. She was rail thin and, if the light hit her hands just right, you could almost see through them, that's how pale she seemed.

Jenny was Erin's older sister and felt like a sister to me as well. Jenny was smart and did well in school and seemed more straight-laced than the rest of us. I don't know how she tolerated us sometimes, because I recall her being the voice of reason amidst our dumb ideas often. That same summer, Jenny took me to my very first music festival, the first ever Vans Warped Tour. We saw Less Than Jake, Blink 182, and The Mighty Mighty Bosstones, among many others. I bought a 7in. vinyl record; one side was Reel Big Fish and the other Goldfinger. Jenny had gotten me my ticket for my birthday, and to this day it's one of the best birthdays I've ever had.

We never knew what it was that the train carried — whether it was people or animals, corporate chain store stock or nothing at all. Our dreams weighed heavy on our fascination with the train. We often talked about where it might be headed. We assumed it was someplace glamorous and sunny, like California. In fact, I think that's the only place we ever named. I guess to a bunch of kids living in a city in the Midwest, California sounds super fucking exciting.

Whenever we heard the whistle of the train in the distance, it was like hearing a call to arms for all dreamers. It was letting us know that we'd better get ready because we were only going to have a short minute to gaze at it and let our imaginations run wild before we lost it in the distance of the night and had to start waiting all over again. The whistle was also our cue to get as close as we dared to those tracks, to feel the breeze of the rushing steel. I was afraid of almost everything back then, including loud noises and my own shadow, so I stood back farther than anyone else.

The train looked rickety and old and I sometimes wondered while standing there if it wasn't going to just give up and lay down off to the side somewhere hoping to be forgotten. It looked as though there wasn't a place in the world it hadn't been, not a single secret it hadn't been told. The train seemed wise. If you listened hard enough, the old wheels running along the rusted tracks would scream songs of many lifetimes at you as it whizzed by — blasting a breeze in your face and making your lungs feel like they could burst at any moment.

The second it was far enough past us in the distance not to be seen anymore, it was time for heartburn, sugar, and caffeine. Sometimes those middle-of-the-night garbage meals at the Fleetwood Diner were the only meal we had all day. Having a good meal usually meant having to head back home and this was not a popular or frequently chosen option for most of us. Especially me. The Fleetwood was an essential part of our late-night ritual because it offered us an open forum of freedom. The diner was open 24 hours a day, seven days a week, and no one ever bothered us about how young we were, whether we should be getting home, or whether we were old enough to be smoking cigarettes. We could sit there for as long as we pleased and feel just like everyone else because *everyone* was there after a long day and it seemed like just about everyone was there because there was nowhere else they had to be.

There were tables inside and outside the diner, and although you could smoke anywhere in the place we always chose to sit outside, even on the colder summer nights that came at the end of the season. Everyone so highly coveted the outdoor tables that you would sometimes wait for a half an hour or even an hour to stake a claim at the first open table. You didn't go to the Fleetwood for the service, and the servers didn't go there because they particularly loved the work, either. It was a grease-pit dive, but it had history, and it was part of our tradition.

I remember one night, after taking in all the chili cheese goodness we could, we ran down to the tracks a couple of blocks down to see again what had been the midnight train, running through downtown. It was our way of saying goodbye to the train, and maybe we knew that at the time and perhaps we didn't.

I distinctly remember standing there and feeling like I felt a shift, some tilt in the universe. After the train was gone for the second time that night, we strolled back up the hill to the diner. All with our arms around each other and our heads leaned against one another's shoulders. I think we all felt something changing — something that wasn't going to be able to go back to normal - and I was uneasy because of it.

The following Fall I was on my way to school and heard a radio report about three Ann Arbor teens — two males and one female — who hopped the midnight train as it passed through downtown. "Those kids actually had the guts to do what we had only *dreamed* of doing," I thought. Only, they ended up in the North End of Flint.

If I remember correctly, the two boys were killed while the girl was forced to watch; the girl was raped, beaten, and left for dead. She survived.

The midnight train wasn't headed for California that night or any other, and it wasn't carrying anyone's hopes or dreams for better days. The train was headed to Hell and we never even knew it. The same hell my parents had gotten me out of years before.

The group had drifted apart at some point toward the end of that summer, without any of us even knowing it. Chris and Rhiannon had broken up by then; Brian was doing whatever it was that he shouldn't have been. Erin just got to be too much for some of us, and I think Jenny and I drifted because eventually Erin and I had a falling out. I became kind of a recluse, hiding out in my bedroom whenever I wasn't at school, with a locked door most of the time to-keep my stepbrothers out. Then I transferred to Stone School that year and eventually, I ended up at Brian and Lynni's all the time.

Life just happened to all of us. I never called any of the group to tell them the news I heard or ask them if they had heard the same – I guess I figured some things were just better left unsaid. I don't know what it would have meant to them to hear the story of the three teens who hopped the train on that ill-fated night. I know that after I heard the story, I lost a part of myself because I lost the feeling I used to get whenever I thought of the train. I stopped dreaming for a while about ever getting out from under the weight of being fifteen and trapped. Occasionally, when I can put out of my mind the story of what really happened, I get lost in the memories of the train, our train, the Midnight Train; the train that delivered you to the front door of your fantasies.

The Tattoo

In February of 2011, I got a large, steam-engine locomotive tattooed on my left leg. I had the work done by Ron Russo of 570 Tattooing Co. in Wilkes-Barre, Pennsylvania. I had wanted the piece done for a long time by then and knew he was the artist to do it. I made an appointment with him while he was at the Motor City Tattoo Expo in Detroit. I spent about 8.5 or 9 hours straight under the needle that day, and it took everything I had in me to get through it. My body started twitching and trembling toward the end.

The damn thing looks like an oil painting on my leg, all black and gray, it's incredible. The number on the locomotive is 28 for two reasons; I was that age when I got the tattoo, for one. The second is that the Tim Barry album, 28th and Stonewall, means the fucking world to me. It was released in 2010, and his song '500 Miles' had gotten me through the trek back home to Michigan from Vermont, where I'd left a relationship I moved there for that blew up in record time. (Two months.) I'm 36 now and not a day goes by that I'm not glad I have the tattoo. I think of my friends and that town and that train close to every single day.

Rhiannon and I are still close like sisters, even though I live in Tennessee and she's still in Michigan. She is married now, to just about the best man I could have ever hoped for her. They have two kids, one boy and one girl, and they still live on the old West Side of Ann Arbor, which is funny to me, because all the time we spent misspending our youth was on the West Side of that damn town, when we weren't in Scio Farms trailer park. Chris is still a fucking hillbilly, he lives in Ohio and he's on social media but that's not to say he's super good at using it. I don't know if he knows that I still think of him as a person that saved my life. But he did, on many levels.

Brian passed away in 2009, on September 11, ironically. I say ironically because that crazy fucker joined the military when we were in our late teens, presumably to avoid going to jail and or prison. The day he graduated from Army Ranger training was the same day that the planes crashed into the twin towers in NYC. He served in Afghanistan and Iraq, for multiple tours of duty, and then stayed on as part of the private security forces in Iraq. He wasn't the same person after the war, but how could he be?

He passed away due to an allergic reaction to medication or something along those lines when he was back home in the States. After the funeral, all the old crew gathered again at the River, along the same ol' railroad tracks we always did. We took a group photograph of the whole crew that day, the last one I have of everyone together.

I did get a chance to thank Brian for all that he and Chris did to protect me from my stepbrothers before he passed away. You see, the butcher knife to my throat was just one of many times my friends tried to intervene where the adults in my life failed me. One day when I was 15 and after my stepbrothers had terrorized my mother and me overnight, drunk and high and violent into the wee hours, my friends took it upon themselves to exact some justice since no one else was protecting me. Chris picked me up and talked my stepbrothers into going out to smoke a joint on some back roads, as he and I would be headed into Ann Arbor from Chelsea.

Once we parked at a smoke spot along the side of the dirt road, Chris pretended like he was looking for some tape to listen to in my stepbrother's Cadillac. He waited until their guard was down, took the keys out of the ignition, and tossed them off into the woods somewhere. We drove off in Chris's car and left them. A short while later, Chris and Brian returned to the spot (leaving me at another friend's house in Scio Farms) and made a mess out of that damn car. They made it clear that it wouldn't be the car the next time they had to intervene.

Erin and Jenny are still out there kicking it, too. Jenny is married with kids of her own and from everything I can see on social media she seems happy. I don't doubt she's a fantastic mom because she always took good care of the rest of the gang and me. Erin is not married and doesn't have kids, but she's been with the same guy for pretty much forever and from what I can tell, she's gained a lot more sense and reason as she's aged. She and I buried the beef we had between us several years ago when we ran into each other as participants at the same fundraising event. Back in 2013 just after I'd moved to Tennessee, my dog, Rosebud, needed emergency surgery to save her life. She had bladder stones blocking her urethra and was headed for kidney failure.

I was hopeless at the time. I'd lost my job in Michigan several months prior and had just relocated to Tennessee for a new job and got laid off after two weeks. I had literally no resources and had to have an online fundraiser to get Rosebud the care she needed. Erin donated, like a fucking angel, reminding me that some ties can't ever be cut, no matter the years or the miles.

That Damned River

I have no fucking idea why the universe has seen fit to bless me with the friends it has. Our crew is a true testament to friendship though, I'll tell you that. The same larger group of folks who spoke of one another as brothers and sisters 15 and 20 years ago still do so today. I wish we got together for weddings and other happy occasions as often as it feels like we get together for funerals.

I recently got the news that two acquaintances from back home in Ann Arbor passed away on the Huron River just a day or two apart. One of them jumped off a trestle over the river by the same damn spot we used to always sit and wait for the train. It was 6:00 am and he was there with a friend; the friend saw him come to the surface and ran to the other side of the bridge to get to him, but he never surfaced again. They didn't find his body for three days, I was told.

The other, an avid fisher-woman, apparently tipped over in her kayak while fishing alone on the river in the early morning hours. It took a day or two before they found her, as well. Same damn river, same damn spot. They both left behind families, including young children.

I never looked at the river or the train the same after I heard that news on the radio about those kids being killed, anyway. As I sit here and reflect while bringing this chapter to a close, I can't help but think that I've finally wrapped my mind around what they mean when they say you can't go home again.

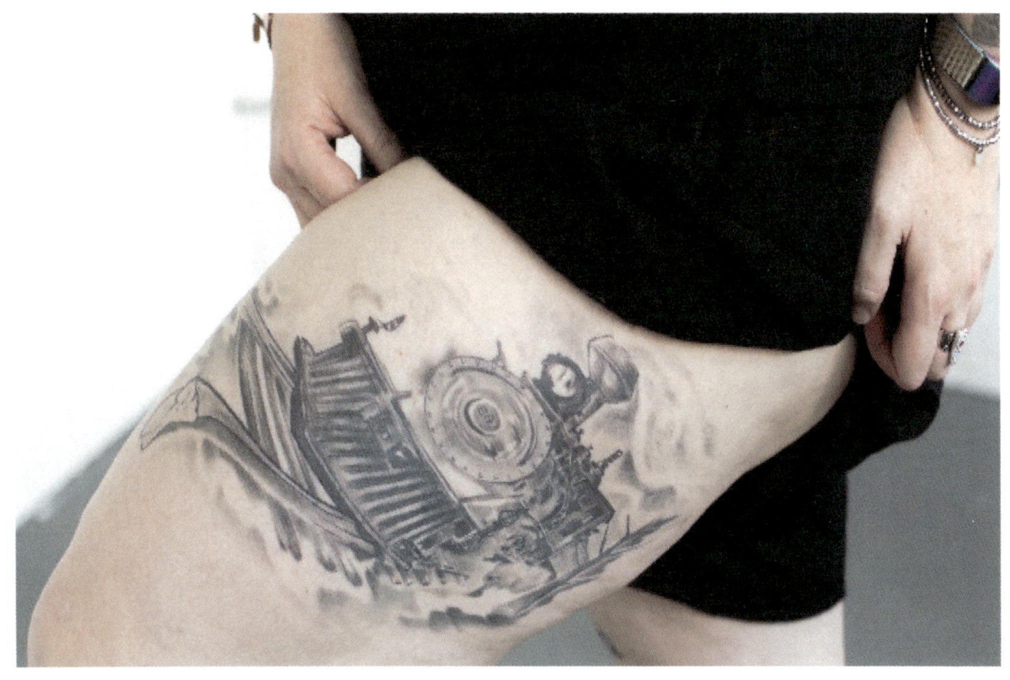

The Midnight Train, done by Ron Russo at the Motor City Tattoo Expo in 2011 when I was 28.

CHAPTER SIX
Salud, Amor, & Pesetas
(Health, Love, & Prosperity)

El Salvador

I visited El Salvador in 2008, part of a study abroad program for graduate school. The experience was life-changing in several ways. The most profound impact it had on me was the realization that, being poor here in the United States is nothing like being poor in other parts of the world. I spent nearly two weeks in a country where people live on an average of $1 a day. Whole families, $1 a day. They are lucky if they eat 600 calories in that day. Yet, the entire time we were there, they asked us for nothing but to share their stories.

"Go home and tell people what you saw here, tell them our stories. Make them understand." They told us this over and over again. It's been ten years and I still haven't gotten many people to understand how good we have it here in the US, in comparison to my friends in El Salvador. Or, why someone from El Salvador would risk so much by coming here illegally to work and build a life that could so easily be ripped away from them in a heartbeat. I can't get most people I know to understand how US foreign policy is destroying the natural resources and economy in El Salvador and creating a lot of the dire circumstances there, forcing people to flee to the very country that has perpetrated so much disaster unto their lives and homes.

The experience was profound, and I dealt with more culture

shock returning home than I'd had upon arriving in San Salvador. It was harder to hear people complaining about things when I got home, knowing how much worse off we could all be. I came to appreciate and treasure resources like clean drinking water and electricity on a whole new level. If I'm being perfectly honest, though, one of the things I appreciated most upon my return was indoor plumbing and the ability to flush waste down the toilet. You don't understand what a luxury that is until you spend a chunk of time having to wipe, pitch the waste in the trash can, and then flush the toilet. I assure you, there's a smell. My friend Cindil and I began to gauge the cleanliness or disaster-level of every public bathroom while traveling on a scale from 1 - El Salvador as a result of this shared experience.

"How's the bathroom?"

"I mean, it's not great, but it's not *El Salvador bad*."

There was a night when the group returned from Ita Maura (the small farm community where we stayed with our host families for part of the trip) and all of us, students and professors alike, shared some drinks on the outdoor patio at the bed and breakfast we stayed in, in San Salvador. At one point that evening our professor Rich gave a toast. "Salud, amor, y pesetas, y tiempo para gozarlos!" Translated roughly, the traditional Latin American toast is, 'To health, love, and prosperity, and the time to enjoy them!' Several of us knew the minute we heard the toast and translation that we wanted to have it done as a tattoo to commemorate the trip.

The Day the Earth Stood Still

It was after my trip to El Salvador in 2008 that I called Angela's (now ex-) husband to tell him that the boys were in danger and needed to get away from her. The night of the great escape, we drove from her parents' house in Chelsea to SC Tattooing in Ann Arbor, where I said my goodbyes to the boys and their dad and hugged them one last time. I walked into the tattoo shop immediately after to get the tattoo of that toast from El Salvador.

Two of my classmates from the trip had come to the tattoo shop that same night, the three of us all getting different versions of the quote tattooed. The words were the same, but placements and font were different for each of us. My classmates left before my tattoo session started and it was just me and Joey and my friend Aaron who had come to hang out and lend moral support for the evening. He knew that saying goodbye to the boys was going to be difficult for me.

Recall that 2008 was an election year in the US, and Barack Obama and Joe Biden with their campaign for 'hope' and 'change' were up against John McCain and Sarah Palin and their campaign for… fuck, I don't even remember. When we were in El Salvador, I remember people there asking us about the upcoming presidential election and for whom we might vote. They were *so afraid* that Obama wouldn't win, and that things would get even worse for them regarding the impact that US foreign policy would have on their resources and economy.

Many emotions were swirling around in me that night as Joey and I were planning my tattoo. We were laughing and purposely pissing off his über conservative stepmom by talking about our plans to vote for Obama and we had tears in our eyes laughing over the latest Dane Cook comedy special, which Joey had playing in the background. Three or four different times Joey drew up the lettering for my tattoo and I found mistaken letters or whatever. At one point he joked, "Fuck. I'm bringing the change to this tattoo!" in reference to the Obama campaign.

Beyond all the laughter and tomfoolery there was a deep sadness. I had a feeling in the pit of my gut that I would never see Angela's boys again, and after spending so much time helping to raise them over the past couple of years, I wasn't sure how I was going to handle that. I wasn't sure what I would do with myself, how I would take up the time that I would usually spend hanging out with them, playing with them, making them meals. I also knew that this would indeed mark the end of my friendship with Angela. Her dad had said to me that night, "I always thought it would be you. With the piercings and the tattoos and weird hair." Meaning that he thought *I* would be the one to end up messed up and on drugs.

I mean, I get that—kind of.

It wasn't me.

It maybe should have been depending on whom you asked, but it wasn't. It was her.

Thankfully I have been allowed to maintain a relationship with Angela's parents, sisters, nieces and nephews, and her ex-husband. I got to speak with the boys on video chat recently. It was the first time I'd seen and talked to them, live and in color, since 2008. They're teenagers now with deep voices and the part of their life that I was in probably doesn't register in their minds very much at all, but I'll never forget them or all that happened back then.

I digress.

With all the emotions running high and the laughter and such, I probably should have known it was a bad time to get a tattoo that involved words that were in Spanish and needed to be spelled correctly. What I ended up with was, 'Salud, Amor, y pesetas, y tiempo para gazarlos.'

That one damn letter has haunted me ever since.

Well, fuck.

It took me about 24 hours to realize that a mistake had been made with my tattoo. I was (maybe unreasonably) embarrassed and at the time couldn't find any humor, not even a little, in becoming one of the biggest tattoo clichés ever: the white girl with a misspelled tattoo in a foreign language. What was I thinking? This was karma, wasn't it!? For all those times I made fun of basic white girls and their tattoos of things like the Rolling Stones' famous lips or the stupid little cherry on their hip bone! I did this to myself. I even attempted to remain in denial about the tattoo being wrong, until I went to a Model United Nations club meeting (don't you dare judge me) where Rich, the professor from El Salvador, spotted and then pointed out the mishap on my leg. It was, by the way, done in giant black letters. I'm talking like 44pt font for fuck's sake.

I wish I could tell you that the misspelling was the only thing about this tattoo that causes it to feel haunting to me, but we're just getting started.

***

In 2010 I returned from Vermont to Michigan after a relationship that I'd relocated for failed in record-breaking time. It was just days before Christmas 2009 when I drove my car with as much as I could fit into it, including my cat Omelet and a lot of hopes and dreams, cross-country. I traveled from Southeast Michigan, through Canada, over the scariest bridges ever in upstate New York, and finally, into St. Albans, Vermont.

I had met the guy, Adrian, on a social networking site called Inked Nation in 2008. Inked Nation was like Facebook for people with tattoos, piercings, and other body modifications as well as artists and practitioners around the globe. It was a place to connect with people with similar interests, stalk the portfolios of your favorite artists around the world, and build your tattoo bucket list. At least, that's what I used it for. I met a few romantic partners and made some great friends on that site that are still in my life today, but the site went down in something like 2009. Inked Nation is also how I found Ron Russo, the artist who did the train on my left leg in 2011.

I left Adrian and drove out of Vermont on February 14 and really had no idea what life was going to be like back in Michigan or how exactly I would rebuild. When I decided to go to Vermont, I gave up a great job that was paying my grad school tuition. I'd also gotten rid of a lot of my furniture and belongings. Whatever I didn't get rid of or couldn't fit in my car had gone into storage. I wasn't sure exactly where I was going to live when I got back. The only smart thing I'd done was to arrange for my graduate courses to be completed online that semester, in part as independent studies, so that I wouldn't lose all of the progress I'd made toward my master's degree.

It took a few months to figure life out but eventually, I did. I stayed with my parents in Michigan for a week or two, then drove down to Tennessee to live in my sister's guest room for a couple of months. I was basically killing time until my new apartment was ready back in Michigan. So long as I was in grad school, I would have some financial aid left over each semester to use for living expenses, so I also had time to look for a job. When I got back to Michigan in the spring of 2010, I moved into an apartment right by Eastern Michigan University's campus that I would share with a friend.

My friends and I picked up right where we'd left off since it had only been, you know, a few fucking months, and I started to feel like me again quickly. I also started dating Brian. *Another* Brian. We'll call him Brian with the Pompadour, to cut down on any confusion.

Brian and I had become friends through Inked Nation back in 2008 and there were mild flirtations but nothing too serious. He had about shit himself when he learned that I'd gone to Vermont, but he was a massive source of support for me when I decided I was heading back home and starting over. We both loved music; specifically, we shared a love for outlaw country and other types of story-telling music as well as everything from John Legend to old gangster rap.

Right around the time that Brian with the Pompadour and I started to become friends, Brian (of the midnight train) and another friend, Pascal, died. Both men had survived multiple tours in Afghanistan and Iraq in the Army and Marines, respectively, and both died from the dumbest shit ever back home. Brian from the reaction to medication and Pascal was struck by a car as he rode his motorcycle home from the gym one night after work. He was working in the Secret Service for the Obama administration at that point.

I had a lot of strong language for God and the universe about those two. Why let them make it home after all of that just to take them out in such lame ways? I felt so *robbed*. Brian with the Pompadour talked me through many a night of deep guttural sobs and seemingly unmanageable sorrow. He showed the same level of support when I left Vermont and returned to Michigan again, permanently. His friendship contributed significantly to the attraction I felt to him romantically.

How a tattoo told me I was pregnant

In the spring of 2010, I'm recovering from the disastrous Vermont relationship and I've moved into my new apartment back in Ypsilanti, preparing for my next semester of graduate school. I had just started dating Brian with the Pompadour. I even found a job, working with my best friend Cindil, running a summer camp at a community center in the hood in Ann Arbor. When I was in high school and hanging out there, the neighborhood was called Stoney Brook, and the ice cream man sold weed and there were drive-by shootings. By the time I started working at the community center the neighborhood was called Bryant, and the City of Ann Arbor had done its best to clean up the reputation.

Starting work at Bryant Community Center was a weird sort of homecoming. The name was different, but I was back in the neighborhood I'd spent much time in as a teenager. Now I was an adult and I was going to be working with this new generation of kids and teens who were, in large part, still just trying to live through and survive the same type of shit that I was back then. I started work there a few weeks before summer camp was set to start, working in the after-school program, getting to know the kids and the lay of the land a bit before summer break started.

I'll never forget my first day on the job, one young lady looked at me and said, "I already like you." I asked her why and she said, "Because you don't act afraid of us like other people do. You just came in and took charge and wouldn't let us get away with stuff." I replied, "That's because I'm not afraid of you... I used to hang out in this neighborhood... and I grew up in Flint." Her eyes got big, like saucers, and I couldn't help but laugh. She never expected that the white lady with tattoos would have come up anywhere like she had. I had immediate street credibility and trust from her, and for the most part, the other kids and teens as well.

Now, for whatever reason, I decided about a week before summer camp started that I would try and fix that tattoo on my leg of the Latin American toast and change the 'a' to an 'o' in "gozarlos" and be done with it. I went to see my friend Joey at his shop and he said we'd start by lightening the letter some, with white ink, which may take a couple of applications, and then go back in with black ink to fix the letter. It sounded reasonable enough to me and he did the first application of white ink right there, on the spot. I remember being surprised at how much more it hurts to go over the old ink than it had to get the damn thing in the first place. Let that be a lesson to you; it hurts much more to tattoo over scar tissue.

When you have a new tattoo, you keep it reasonably moist with some kind of healing salve. For me back then it was Aquaphor. So usually, you keep the stuff applied to the tattoo and once or twice a day, depending on your lifestyle and what you and your tattoo are exposed to, you wash the tattoo and reapply. After a few days, there's a very thin, flaky scab that starts to form on the tattoo. As it continues to heal that scab begins to peel, or fall off, especially whenever you apply the salve. Usually, this is around the time the damn thing itches to hell.

After I'd gotten that little bit of white ink over that letter, and was working the summer camp at Bryant, I noticed that the tattoo was acting funny. The scab was thick, and weird, and not at all like a normal tattoo scab. It sure as hell wasn't flaking off, and I could tell that if I tried to pull it off, it would bleed and scar. I didn't want to get in the public pool with the kids in summer camp because I wasn't sure exactly what was going on. The scab didn't look white, either, like the color of the ink, which is what they usually do. Instead, it looked like a strange, almost yellow color.

Cindil and I talked about it one day, and she wondered if maybe the tattoo was infected. That didn't make any sense; it wasn't red or hot around the tattoo. I washed it and kept it moist with the goopy-ass Aquaphor and started running through the list of other possibilities. I wondered, was I rejecting the tattoo? It had never happened before but that didn't mean it couldn't happen. I started to think of all the reasons that I knew why a tattoo would reject.

I'd been told that sometimes ink from a tattoo might get pushed out, or the body may reject it because a person has antibiotics in their system. That didn't apply; I hadn't been on any antibiotics. I'd been told that some people have allergic reactions to tattoo ink, but that didn't make sense either. The only tattoos that ever itched excessively on me were ones with red in them, and this was just plain white. Not a lot of pigment there. It also didn't itch. It just looked funny. Suddenly it dawned on me. Someone had told me once at the tattoo shop that tattoos might reject if a person was pregnant. I have no idea if this is scientific fact, but it's what I knew to be true at the time, and I got worried.

I don't remember how much time elapsed between when I had the thought about the possibility of being pregnant and when I actually took the pregnancy test. I was sitting at the bar that separated my kitchen and dining room one evening after work and suddenly it occurred to me that I'd also been losing a lot of hair when I would get out of the shower and comb it out. This was another thing I'd heard could happen when a woman is pregnant. I decided I should probably take a pregnancy test.

I headed to my friend Noelle's apartment to take the test, I didn't want to be alone depending on the results. I remember offering the disclaimer that I was probably freaking out for no reason. I'd been on birth control for years and never had a pregnancy before, so it was probably just stress or something. But, I said, I'd better take the test just to be safe.

When I said from the bathroom that the test was positive, Noelle said, "That's not funny."

I wasn't joking.

I had just spent my last $7 on that fucking pregnancy test. That's how broke I was after the cross-country move to Vermont, back from Vermont, the travel and extended stay in Tennessee, and the first and last month's rent and deposit required to move into my place. I hadn't gotten a summer camp paycheck yet. I wanted to take a second test to be sure, but I didn't even have the money to buy another. Noelle offered to buy it and off to Target we went.

We returned to Noelle's apartment a short time later.

I was still pregnant.

This wasn't good news.

So, what now?

I texted Brian with the Pompadour and asked him if I could drive out and meet up with him after work, I needed to talk to him. He lived about a 45-minute drive away, which meant I had plenty of time to have the worst butterflies of my life in my stomach, trying to figure out how I was going to tell him I was pregnant. As an extra fun bonus, because life works in seriously fucking weird ways, my phone rang while I was driving. It was Adrian in Vermont.

That was the last thing I needed.

I met up with Brian and we drove around Jackson, Michigan. He was driving my car and we'd just gotten gas and cigarettes. By this point, I wanted to throw up and I couldn't figure out how to tell him. Finally, I said, "So, a funny thing happened today...turns out, I'm pregnant."

"No," he replied.

"Yes," I said.

"No," he said again.

"Yes," I responded.

He said, "That's out of control."

I responded, "I'm going to need you to use adult words and have an actual response to this shit because I'm freaking the fuck out."

That night and the following days are somewhat of a blur. I didn't drive home until like two o'clock in the morning that night, knowing that I had to get up and be to work by 9 am. I remember crying a lot. I also remember telling him that if he wasn't absolutely and completely on board with having a baby, that I didn't want to have it. I had seen what life was like for friends and relatives who dealt with deadbeat baby daddies. Hell, I'd seen some of my friends over the years *be* deadbeat baby daddies. I wasn't interested in forcing someone to have a child they didn't want and then living the rest of my life battling resentment, anger, and refusal to contribute to the child's life, financially or otherwise. There were other things to consider as well.

I would be coming to the end of my final semester of graduate school, getting ready to write my Capstone and graduate, around the time I'd have been due to have the baby. I'd been drinking *a lot* the past few months after leaving Vermont and beginning to date Brian. It had been a really fucking hard and confusing time and drinking was way more fun than sitting around wallowing in self-pity or regret.

I was also on medication for depression and anxiety, and if I decided to carry a baby to term, I knew I'd have to stop taking that medication. I knew what life looked like for me without medication because I'd tried it before. It didn't go well. I'll just tell you that. My job with the community center was only temporary, for the duration of summer, and in a few weeks, I'd be out of a job with no prospects for a new job. I also didn't have health insurance.

I'd always said that if I was going to be a mom, I'd want to be the kind of mom I had. I wanted to be home where I could spend the most quality time with my kid(s) and be involved in their school life, know their friends, etc. A single mom with over $150,000 in debt from college and graduate school, no job, and no health insurance was not exactly a recipe for success. So, a few days later, when Brian told me that he didn't want to have a baby, that if we were to have a baby together he hoped it would be after a long-term relationship and not after just two or three months of dating, the decision was made.

I exercised my right to choose.

Deciding not to have a baby was the most difficult decision I've ever faced. I've always believed in every woman's right to choose whether she becomes a mother, but I'd always hoped I could avoid having to make that choice for myself. The following weeks were fucking brutal. I still had to get through summer camp and act like every-thing was normal, prepare for and have the abortion, and figure out what was going to happen as far as employment and keeping a roof over my head were concerned. I was also taking graduate courses that summer.

It was a Friday - August 12, 2010 - when I terminated the pregnancy. Brian was not at the clinic with me, he spent the day working, but my mom sat by my side the whole day. I had decided to have a medical abortion rather than a surgical abortion. When I was 15, I had held a friend's hand while she had a surgical abortion. I could never get the painful sounds she made and how she cried and squeezed my hand out of my head. That was why I decided on a medical abortion.

When I was finished at the clinic I drove out and picked up Brian who had completed his day at work and returned home to face the most heartbreaking weekend of my life. He did his best to think of things to keep me distracted and cared for while my body did its job. He brought a multi-disc DVD set of the show The Munsters among others. I still have trouble watching that show, when it had once been a favorite. The experience was painful and bloody, and I still don't know what's worse – a medical or surgical abortion.

The Aftermath

The abortion impacted me for a long time and still does affect me. It's not because I feel like I should have had a baby back then, the bottom line is I couldn't have cared for a child well. I also think that, sometimes, being a good parent means recognizing when you *can't* or *won't* be a good parent. What has continued to impact me the most over all these years is the shame attached to having an abortion. For me, that shame comes from the broader debates about what abortion does or does not mean and the moral implications of having one.

I remember calling one of my oldest and dearest friends, Amber, when I'd decided to abort my pregnancy. Through tears I asked her if she thought that there was a Hell, and if there was, would I go to it because I got an abortion. It was heavy shit. I realized recently that even though 1 in 3 women have an abortion, I was still allowing myself to feel like it was a disgraceful thing. I was forcing myself to hide, to feel shame and guilt, allowing myself to think of me as *less than* because of it. Less than worthy, less wholesome than other women, less than myself. I still haven't fixed the tattoo, because I wanted to avoid thinking about it as much as possible.

I've treated my abortion like this dirty little secret for so long that it's gotten in the way of me doing things like writing this book, advocating for women's reproductive rights, or offering comfort to other women who are facing the same choice I did. So, I decided that I had to write about it. Other women out there that I don't even know yet are going to read my story and need to see this.

So…hey.

You.

Yeah…you.

I'm here.

It was hard, and it sucked and some people are going to judge me, but that's ok. I'm still here. I hope other women see this and that they know that they're not the worst person ever, either. You're *not* the most despicable woman who ever lived. You made the choice that was right for you for whatever reasons existed for you at the time.

Ok?

Ok.

Let's move on, together. <3

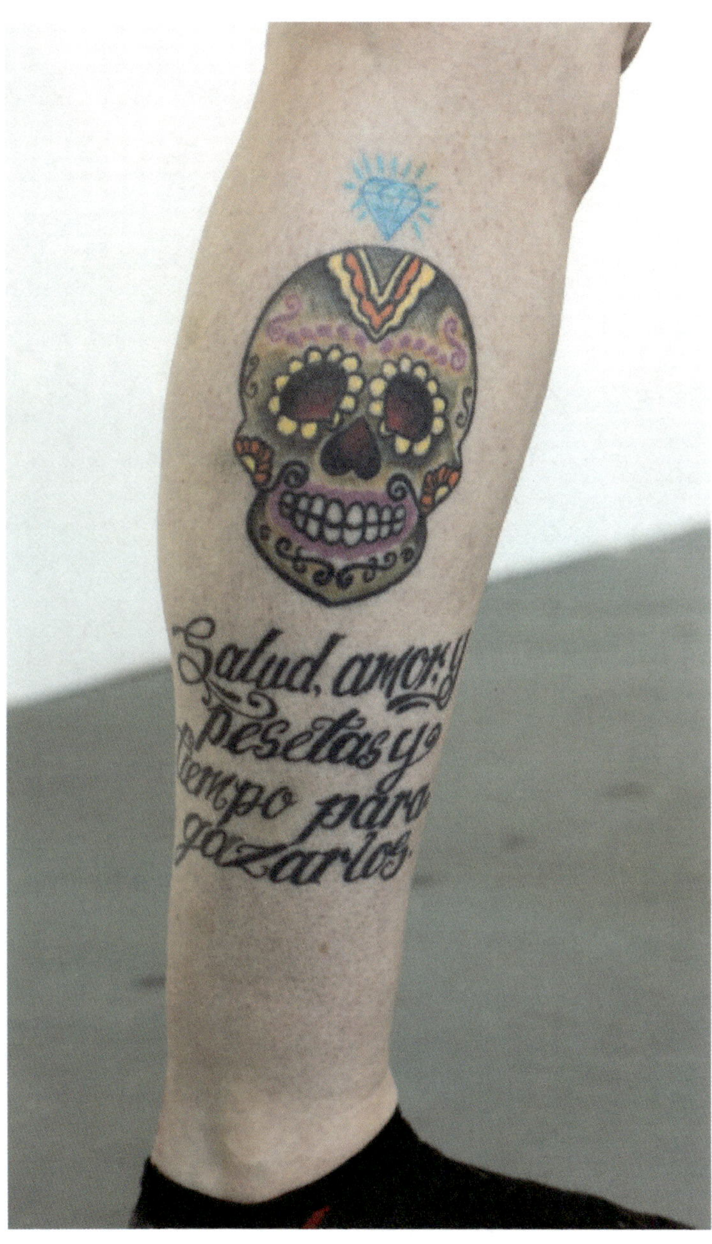

Traditional Latin American toast tattoo, done by Joey Singleton at SC Tattooing & Body Piercing in Ann Arbor, Michigan. Completed in 2008 at age 25. Still not fixed.

CHAPTER SEVEN

The Sleeve, Part 1: Family

Everything starts somewhere.

I was four years old when my dad died. He was 52. We were both too young. As a result of his untimely passing, I grew up with a sense that something was missing. That some part of me, of who I was, was missing. It's a feeling that is always sort of just hanging out inside of me whether I'm consciously aware of it or not.

Am I like him?

Did I inherit this from him?

Did he like this kind of music, too?

These are the kinds of questions that popped into my mind frequently as I was growing up, and still sometimes do.

The idea for my sleeve started with a photograph of my father. But it wasn't just any photograph. I was around 13 when my oldest sister blurted out, drunk, that my dad had been in prison. I was stunned. I vaguely recalled hearing something about this when I was in grade school, but I couldn't quite put all the pieces together in my mind. *"What do you mean, dad was in prison?"* I asked.

She told me that he'd robbed a liquor store or something with a couple of friends. He'd maintained his innocence up to his death, saying that he had been in the wrong place at the wrong time. I eventually worked up the nerve to ask my aunts and uncles about it, which was especially awkward because there was an eight-and-a-half-year gap between the time that my dad passed away and when we got to see his side of the family again.

My uncle Jim, Dad's younger brother, explained the background to me. Their father, my grandfather, had died when dad was about seventeen. My dad went into the Navy to try and help support the family: his mom and four siblings. It was while my dad was in the Navy that he ended up on the wrong side of the law.

According to what my uncle said, Dad was one of the only guys in his group of friends who had a car. One night, while on base, his buddies asked him for a ride to the liquor store. Dad agreed to give them a ride and is said to have stayed out in the car smoking a cigarette while the other guys went in. According to my uncle, the guys came out and got in the car and dad drove off. The rest of the night was normal until they were pulled over and subsequently arrested for armed robbery. The guys got something like twenty dollars out of the robbery.

My dad's sentence was twenty years-to-life, and he served ten, to the best of anyone's recollection.

As a young adult, I became obsessed with learning more about the case and the guys who were arrested with my dad. Was my dad innocent? I was in college when I finally worked up the nerve to call Kentucky's Department of Corrections, where he'd been incarcerated in federal prison.

The only information I had for the request was his birth date and social security number, which I'd gotten off some military test records that my uncle Pete had sent me the year before. My heart was pounding and my voice was shaking during that call. I think I got lucky that day because the woman on the other end of the line was an absolute angel.

I explained the situation to her and told her that I'd heard he'd served his sentence in Kentucky. I went on to explain that I wanted to see if I could get copies of court records and anything else related to the case. It was 2004 when I made that call, and my dad was arrested in 1956, so I wasn't sure what to expect. She couldn't find anything in their electronic records so she said she was going to look through the archives and call me back. I was somewhat skeptical that I would hear back.

She did call back, though, to say that she'd found his records! She sounded nearly as excited as I was. His records were somewhere in the basement, buried in an old filing system in the archives. Included in the files were pictures from his arrest and release. She told me it would cost me ten cents for every page copied, plus postage. I sent a money order for a couple of dollars. Then I waited.

The first time I ever saw his face

Until the moment that I opened the envelope from the Kentucky Department of Corrections, I'd only ever seen photographs of my dad as a middle-aged man. All of our family photos with him were from when my sister Sara and I were babies, or right before we were born. When I opened that envelope and saw what was inside, my breath caught in my throat and I started crying.

The lovely lady at the Kentucky Department of Corrections had included photocopies of my dad's arrest records and a copy of his release photo from the 1960s. But above and beyond all of that she included the *original copy* of his intake photograph; the picture was taken in 1956 when my dad was first arrested. He had a greased back pompadour and wasn't wearing glasses. He looked just like a James Dean or Johnny Cash.

"I look like my dad," I thought.

My whole life I'd been told that I looked just like my mother, and I do, but no one ever said anything about looking like my dad. When I looked down into my hands at that photo, I could see my lips, nose, and the shapes of my eyes. Well, kind of. I could kind of see the shapes of my eyes. The photo is black and white so his eyes have shadows over them. I looked though, at that moment, and saw those pieces of me staring back up at me. I couldn't stop crying. I finally felt like I knew him in a way that I hadn't before. I knew right then that I would get that photograph tattooed on myself somewhere. It would be years later, during graduate school, that I finally did. And that's where the idea for the sleeve began.

Dad's Portrait

The inspiration behind my sleeve was that it would represent people of great import in my life. The family members and friends who have been my beacons of light, guiding me back to myself and home, wherever that is, whenever I've needed it. I enlisted the help of my friend and tattoo artist, Larry, who specializes in portrait work. I decided to go with a neo-traditional, Sailor Jerry-inspired theme for my sleeve because when my dad's photograph was taken he had been in the Navy.

The first part of my sleeve was dad's portrait. It was placed on the flat side of my forearm. His face is in blacks and grays just like the photograph and is framed by a length of rope and three roses. The three roses represent me and my two sisters, my dad's three daughters. My oldest sister has a different father biologically, my mom's first husband, but my dad adopted her and gave her his last name.

I've been told more times than I can count that all my dad ever wanted in life was a family, a wife, and kids of his own. His first wife, I've heard, was unable to have children and they had a miserable marriage wherein she cheated on him regularly. When he met my mom at The Shop (that's what we've always called the different factories in Flint) and fell in love with her it was the start to all his dreams coming true. As far as he was concerned, all three of us girls were his daughters.

The Father's Day before my dad died, we went shopping for him and his garden. We bought him a large bench swing made of rustic logs and three rose bushes. Each of us girls picked out a different color rose. When Dad fell ill and eventually moved to my aunt and uncle's house, his rose bushes and swing were moved to their yard as well. I can remember sitting with dad on that swing, in the shade of a large tree at Evie and Jim's. When he passed, his remains were cremated and were spread over those rose bushes. The roses in my tattoo match the color of the rose bush that I chose for my dad as a gift that year, tea roses.

My Mom, My Anchor

I was bullied relentlessly in high school. So much so that I transferred out of Chelsea High School. It wasn't just name-calling and rumor spreading that I dealt with in Chelsea. I was physically assaulted on more than one occasion. The most remarkable of which was when the quarterback of the football team threw a block of ice at my face, hitting me square between the eyes. He knocked me unconscious, blackening both of my eyes and leaving a welt across the span of my forehead. That was just one of the many straws that broke the camel's back and was the catalyst for me getting the hell out of that school system altogether and transferring to Stone School in Ann Arbor.

I graduated high school when I was 16 because of the way the credit system was structured at Stone and because I was doing anything I could to avoid being at home with my stepbrothers. I volunteered for every campus job I could get, racked up community service hours, and took all the extra classes I could. Unfortunately, my ambition backfired.

At 16, I was smart enough, but not emotionally prepared to go to college. I graduated high school in June of 1999, turned 17 that August, and started college in September. Nineteen-ninety-nine was the same year that I was partying my face off with Angela and the meth heads, the crazy ex-boyfriend(s), and so on. It should come as no surprise that I flunked out of my first semester at Washtenaw Community College. I flunked out with real pizzazz. My GPA was a staggering 1.1. I spent the next several months self-medicating by way of booze and partying with Angela. If I'm being honest, I was scared shitless to go back and try again.

One day my mom asked me if I wanted to go to lunch. I said sure. My mom still owned the house in Chelsea at this point and my stepbrothers were finally gone. It made it easier for me to spend time around home. Going out to lunch was a special treat. She didn't take me to lunch that day, though, not at first. She fucking tricked me.

She drove to the same community college I'd flunked out of months before, told me I was too damn bright to waste it, walked me into the student services building and straight over to the counseling office. She informed the receptionist that we needed an appointment with a guidance counselor *immediately* and that we'd wait in the lobby until one was available. My mom doesn't play.

That was the day I re-enrolled in classes at Washtenaw Community College (WCC) and the day that I met Cole. Cole was my guidance counselor at WCC, but he was also a mentor and a significant influence on my life. I cried so many times in his office, starting with that first day I met him, telling him that I was afraid I was going to fuck up again. Every semester, though, Cole was there cheering me on and making sure I knew what classes to take next. When I accepted a scholarship for my academic performance, he was there. When I graduated with my Associates in Arts, he was there.

I would learn many years after the fact that Cole was actually a fugitive of more than forty years and that his real name was Ronald Bridgeforth. He'd been featured on America's Most Wanted in the nineties and had been on the FBI's Most Wanted list for decades for jumping bail on charges of Assault with a Deadly Weapon on a San Francisco police officer in a shootout in 1968. He turned himself in at the age of 67. However, none of that is consequential to me. He's still one of the most exceptional people I've ever known, and I still love him. That man helped keep me from throwing my life away on fear and recklessness.

Mom did take me to lunch after the business of enrolling me in classes was handled. We went to a place called Memphis Smokehouse Blues. That became a tradition for my mom and me. Every time there was something to celebrate or work through, every significant milestone commemorated, was followed by a meal at the Smokehouse.

I digress.

On the opposite side of my arm from dad's portrait is an anchor with a large heart and a banner that reads, "Mom." I have always said that throughout much of my life, my mom has been my anchor in life's stormy waters. We have had more than our fair share of difficulties, resentments, and battles fought against each other. We would fight like nobody's business in my teen years. We'd scream until our voices cracked. But in the end, she's the person who I always look to for comfort and sanity in the middle of an insane and senseless world. She understands me as nobody else does.

Without my mom I'm quite confident I would never have made it to the right high school, and likely would have dropped out. I might never have gone back to college out of fear of failure, would have given up dreaming about being a writer before I ever even started. So much of my life has been chaos and confusion. My mom is the one constant.

She was right, by the way, about me being too bright to waste it. Eventually, I got my Bachelor's of Science in Political Science and became the first person (and still the only person) in my family to earn a graduate degree. I hold a Master's in Public Administration.

The Judith Ann

My aunt Judy has always been a large part of my life. She was sort of like a second mom to us as kids and spoiled us rotten whenever she could. She also did a lot of behind-the-scenes work that I really wasn't entirely aware of until recently. I remember her taking us shopping for clothes sometimes, especially for new school clothes. She once took us to a boutique that was my first run-in with high-end, couture fashion. The blue jeans had all kinds of leopard print patches and fancy bobbles and fringe accoutrements on them and one pair was like $100. I will admit that I still don't really 'get' fashion. I certainly don't get why a fucking pair of jeans should cost $100.

Aunt Judy is also responsible for my sister Sara's and my first big concert, New Kids on the Block, and a trip to the restaurant that rotates in Detroit. I think I was seven. I remember making my first call from a cellular car phone with Aunt Judy. You know, like the *actual* car phone, built into and attached to the car. I think she let me call my mom. I felt like I lived in the future.

I remember one New Year's Eve, staying with Aunt Judy in some fancy hotel with indoor put-put golf. I was shook. Who knew places like this existed in real life?! I felt like Tom Hanks in the movie Big. I found out a couple of years ago that Aunt Judy helped make my trip to Sea World for my 12th birthday happen too. It was my dream trip because I was in love with dolphins and whales and wanted to be a marine biologist when I grew up. My mom said I leaned in so close to pet the dolphins she thought she was going to have to jump in and fish me back out of the tank.

Even in adulthood, Aunt Judy always lets me know she's there, just like she did throughout my childhood. And not just for me, but for my friends, too. She's donated to GoFundMe campaigns for me and at least two of my friends when our fur babies were in grave danger. Once she gave to a campaign to help one of my very best, ride-or-die friends get home safe and away from an abusive relationship. She's the kind of aunt I try to be.

She also happens to be named for a ship. I'd been carrying that information around in the back of my head for years when I started working on the sleeve. I figured, what better way to honor Aunt Judy than by having a Sailor Jerry ship on my bicep? In the process of writing this book I reached out to her to ask if she knew why she was named after a ship. She said that from what she remembers when my grandmother was pregnant with her, my grandfather took the family to Port Huron to watch the boats out on the water. While there, a particularly large and beautiful ship sailed by, named Judith Ann. My grandmother proclaimed, "If I have a baby girl, I'll name her Judith Ann."

She noted that my grandfather drove his pregnant wife and three children under the age of five, five hours to watch the boats at Port Huron. My Papa is clearly a courageous man. And if you know anything about sibling rivalry, then it probably doesn't surprise you to know that Judy, the youngest of all of her siblings, *loves* to point out to my mom that her tattoo is bigger than my mom's tattoo.

Yep, she fucking measured it.

The Turquoise Butterfly

Honestly, I'm lucky that my sister and I didn't manage to kill each other when we were growing up. Sibling rivalry is one thing, but there was violence between us. I was around eight or nine years old when mom declared that unless someone was bleeding or dying, she didn't care if Sara and I were fighting. She didn't want to hear it. That's how much we fought. The first real injury I remember getting from Sara was a shard of glass going into my palm, and nesting itself into my hand (it's still buried in there) when I was three or four years old. This was followed by splitting my upper lip wide open by way of throwing a wooden swing at my face.

Things didn't improve as we got older. There were fist fights. I even pulled a butcher knife on her. Once when a group of us were playing tackle football in the backyard, I accidentally poked her in the eye. To return the favor, she backhanded me so hard that she dislocated my shoulder and knocked me out. When I came to, she was standing over me waiting to say, "Don't you dare tell mom." I waited until the next day when my shoulder popped loudly in class and the teacher saw the bruise and called my mom. On our way to the emergency room that afternoon my mom stopped at home to leave a note for Sara that read, "Taking your sister to the ER and I **am not** happy about it." For three years in high school, my sister and I didn't even speak — she told people I died. I narced on her to my mom about some big stuff, during one of those "Be more like your sister!" screaming matches, and that was that.

Somewhere around the age of 21, all the beef between us was dropped and Sara and I began to grow close. She really looked out for me in many ways. The older we got, the more often she stepped in as a nurturing influence, supporting me as I survived college and then grad school. She moved to Wisconsin in 2006 with her boyfriend (now husband) Sam and being farther apart, in some ways, brought us closer together. We had regular chats on the phone and when I graduated from college and was having a hard time financially, Sara and Sam would do things like surprising me with grocery store gift cards.

During the time when my niece was shuffling from my house to Angela's and I found myself in a relationship with one of the world's finest drunks and emotional succubae, I got sick. Like, *really* sick. I had a shake that I couldn't control and I was throwing up all the time. Even when I was just upset and crying, it would make me throw up. I would sometimes stutter, which had never happened before. I was dropping weight because I didn't have much of an appetite and couldn't keep anything down when I did.

I had the world's worst job as a patient transporter at St. Joseph Mercy Hospital in Ypsilanti at the time, and I was missing *a lot* of work because of my illness as well as rampant depression and anxiety. I was only 25 years old and the doctors thought it was possible that I had the same type of cancer that killed my dad — esophageal cancer. I had an endoscopy and colonoscopy on the same day.

The doctors told my mom that there was nothing wrong with me, physically. Whatever was going on with me had to be stress because my insides were perfectly healthy. It would still take several weeks, maybe a couple of months, before I admitted to anyone that I was living in a horribly abusive relationship with a fucking emotional terrorist. I didn't have to tell my sister Sara, though, she just knew.

I lost my job at the hospital for missing too much work during my probationary period of employment, and she called me immediately the same day. She and Sam offered to fly me out to Wisconsin for a break, to clear my head a bit. What did it matter since I wasn't working anyway? Sara knew *something* was going on and she also knew that she probably wouldn't get it out of me unless I got away and spent some time with her in person.

I wrote a letter to the abusive boyfriend before I left, told him to get out of my apartment and not be there when I got home. To his credit, he wasn't there when I got back. However, he stole a bunch of my shit and did asshole things like steal all of the batteries out of my remotes and take light bulbs out of light fixtures. He threatened both to take or kill my cat, but he didn't. I remember driving home with my parents from the airport, thinking I might throw up the whole way there, worrying about whether or not Omelet (my cat) was dead in my apartment. Or gone.

I had the locks changed immediately after getting back to the apartment and had come clean with my family about what had been going on for the past several months. Anything my ex-boyfriend left behind ended up in a dumpster, thrown out by myself and two dear friends, Brad and Bridget. Brad was singing (to the tune of Beyoncé's song, 'To the Left, to the Left'), "To the left, to the left. Everything you own in the dumpster to the left," the whole time and I was laughing myself to tears.

My health rebounded immediately with my ex-boyfriend gone and I started laughing and enjoying life again. I also applied for and was accepted into a Master's Degree program a short time later. That was the first time my sister saved me from an asshole, and it wouldn't be the last. It was definitely a turning point in my relationship with her, where I knew beyond a doubt that she had my back and always would, as did Sam, whom she married in 2009. I got to be in the wedding party. I also got to give the Maid of Honor's toast because the actual Maid of Honor was nervous. (No pressure, write a toast for your older sister's wedding while you stuff your face with food, and have about ten minutes until show time.)

My sister loves butterflies, so a butterfly seemed like the best way to honor her in my sleeve. Larry really knocked it out of the park because the damn thing looks like a piece of turquoise jewelry. Like a pendant that belongs on a necklace. It's one of maybe three tattoos that hurt enough to make me want to cry — it's in the elbow pit. I joked about how it must be payback for all the shit I did to piss my sister off when we were kids. That, *of course*, it would be her tattoo would hurt that much.

Note: All of the tattoos in my sleeve were completed by Larry Shelby of Empire Tattoo in Redford, Michigan, over a span of years from 2008 – 2012.

Portrait of my dad completed in 2008. Based on the reference of his prison intake photo taken in 1956.

Mom anchor, completed in 2009.

Judith Ann ship, in tribute to my aunt Judy. Completed in 2009.

Turquoise butterfly, in tribute to my older sister, Sara. Completed in 2009.

CHAPTER EIGHT

The Sleeve, Part 2: Framily

Framily are the people that are your chosen family. They may know you better than your blood relatives, and you might trust them more deeply. In my world, they are also known as "Ride or Dies," "Besties for the Resties," and "BFFs." I'm being silly, but I'm also serious. Framily is made up of the people that you don't know how to walk the earth without, the brothers and sisters who don't share any blood relation but for whom you'd at least *consider* hiding evidence.

Based solely on my own life experience, it seems that my generation is among the first to stop with that old, "blood is thicker than water," adage and accepts that just because people are related to you doesn't mean they aren't assholes. Say what you want about Millennials, but some of this shit we just have a better handle on than Baby Boomers and Gen Xers. Further, we seem to be the first generation to accept that if you *are* related to an asshole, especially if they're the kind of asshole that is abusive or takes advantage of you, it is absolutely acceptable to tell them to fuck off out of your life. Hence my sleeve is made up of nearly equal parts family and framily.

Mark David Kidd

My friend Mark was unlike anyone else I've ever met. He grew up in a hyper-religious and conservative family but was one of the most open-minded and accepting people I've ever known. He was a Marine, and by the time I met him he had served two tours in Iraq as part of Operation Iraqi Freedom. He'd also been in a serious relationship with a registered member of the Communist Party, which always cracked me up.

We met when I was an undergrad. I was working as an assistant to Dr. Krause, a professor in the Political Science Department at Eastern Michigan University. Dr. Krause was born with short arms and legs, a result of the thalidomide tragedy[1]. He walked on seemingly uncomfortable prosthetic limbs that were stiff almost like stilts.

As his assistant, it was my job to anticipate Dr. Krause's needs before he did. I would run around campus to collect books and other research materials, help carry his things to class, and make sure that the classroom technology was working like it was supposed to. It was in one of his classrooms that I first met Mark Kidd.

For the record, I thought Mark was a total jackass on first sight. He wore tweed suit jackets with suede elbow patches to school *every day.* He laughed at his own jokes—a lot. I was perpetually rolling my eyes at him. I also wasn't impressed by the Marine thing — I *hated* the war in Iraq. I was scared to death of losing my friends who were on active duty overseas throughout the conflict.

But Mark always had thoughtful questions and responses to lectures which intrigued me about him. After a while, I softened up. I ended up taking an international law class held by the drunkest professor ever to hold tenure, and Mark also happened to be in it as well.

Mark took a real liking to Dr. Krause, and between his budding friendship with me and his interest in talking with Dr. Krause, he was always hanging around the Political Science Department, usually driving me bananas and challenging me in ways that I didn't want to be challenged. Whenever I was winning an argument he would end it with, "Woman! Go make me a pie!" That was his way of saying that women belonged in the kitchen, which was absolutely a joke; he didn't think like that at all. That's why it was funny. And

[1]Thalidomide was a medication prescribed to pregnant women in some parts of the world from 1958-1961. The medication was supposed to be harmless and was prescribed to relieve morning sickness. However, approximately 2,000 babies were born were severe congenital disabilities as a result of the medication, and about half of those babies died within months.

infuriating. Mark also fucking *loved* pie of any kind, so he always hoped I'd give in one day and bake one.

I knew there was something incredibly special about Mark when, in the winter months, he began protecting Dr. Krause's parking spot outside of the building where his office and classrooms were located. Idiot students who were too lazy to park and walk would always steal his spot which would cause serious problems with him getting to class on time. It was also very dangerous because the ice and snow did not mesh well with his stiff, metal prostheses.

When Mark found out that this was happening recurrently he began coming to campus early every morning. He would haunt the parking spot in the cold Michigan winter temperatures and yell at anyone who tried to steal it. Then he'd walk Dr. Krause inside once he had arrived and parked safely.

Mark had served two tours by the time I met him. The story goes that Mark was on his way home from his first tour of duty when he found out that his friend and fellow Marine had a pregnant wife at home — she'd become pregnant when her husband was home on a brief leave. Mark didn't feel good about his friend going back to the front lines when he had a child on the way, so Mark went to the commanding officer and demanded to take his place. The other guy went home to his family and Mark served his second tour, then came back home and started college.

Mark had a lot of guilt about being safe at home when so many of his brothers-in-arms were still out there fighting. He was taking twenty-one credit hours per semester, which is an insane number of classes to take. Mark was determined, though, to get done with school and get back out into the world and do some good. To try to make up for some of the ugliness he saw while overseas.

Mark and I both had this feeling burning inside our guts, telling us that we were supposed to be changing the world for the better. I wanted to go to developing countries and study the varying cultures and legal systems and try and impact how Americans perceived these places. I also wanted to work here in the United States, in human and civil rights, focusing on working with American Indians and in the criminal justice system.

Mark said he wanted to help form democratic governments in other countries. He thought whatever we did, we should do together because he said that my heart was too big and the world too ugly of a place. He looked me in the face one day and said, "Kelly, I've seen what people are capable of doing to one another, it's heartbreaking. Your heart is so big and so fragile, I can't let you go out there and face all of that alone."

Sometime late in 2006, Mark got a call from the Marines. They asked if he would be willing to come back on active duty and serve another tour. They were desperate for more people. He told me that if he didn't, someone else would have to, so he agreed to go. I was terrified in a way that made me push him away in the weeks leading up to his departure. I drove him away so that I wouldn't feel abandoned by him.

Eventually, I got over myself, and I wrote him a long letter on Myspace (fuck, I'm old) and told him I was sorry and wanted to see how he was doing. From September 2006 through January 2007, Mark and I wrote each other as much as possible. He also posted blogs occasionally about what was on his mind. On January 9, 2007, he sent me an email I'll never forget. I still have it saved on my computer.

> I am planning to move somewhere around Ypsilanti if I can find some place that meets my very stringent criteria, cheap. So, keep your eyes out for a good place that I could move into around May if you don't mind. I don't think that I want to move into my old place it wasn't worth the money that they wanted for it. I'll bet that I can find another place in the area for around the same amount but nicer. By nicer I mean hooker free, I know that we are talking about Ypsilanti and I must expect some but at least none selling their products in front of my house.
>
> I will not be able to get on-line too often now. They are sending me to a new place that doesn't have any internet. I am not looking forward to going there. It's in the middle of the city and I will be interacting with the people every day. That is good for

> learning about the culture but bad for the whole staying away from people shooting at me. I counted it out and I only have about 95 days left here. I'm over the hump now.
>
> Well I have got to get going so take care and have a good next semester. I will give you more updates next time I can get online. Mark

On January 25, 2007, my dear friend, Corporal Mark David Kidd, was shot down by Sniper fire in Al Anbar Province, Iraq. He succumbed to his wounds. I got the call from Dr. Krause when the news hit stateside. I was sitting in my living room, getting directions to my friend Dixon's sister's house to help plan for *his* funeral, when I got the call about Mark.

Devastated is an understatement.

That week was fucking heavy in a way I've never really recovered from.

In April 2007, I walked in my graduation commencement and received my diploma, a Bachelor's in Science. Mark should have been with me. When it came time to put my sleeve together, I felt like Mark was too big and important to be summed up by any one symbol. I really had a hard time figuring it out. I looked up traditional tattoo meanings and saw that swallows were often used to symbolize a sailor's experience on a ship, and/or a fallen sailor's soul being carried to Heaven. If anyone I know is in Heaven, it's Mark. So, I have a swallow carrying a banner that simply says, "Mark" over my dad's portrait and next to my sister's butterfly.

The Sextant

For this book, I'm going to call the person who inspired the sextant tattoo, "X."

I met X when I was 14 years old. A mutual friend, Ben, would do random shit like call or show up at my house in the middle of the night to sneak out and hang out and be up to, mostly, no good.

One night he showed up with X in the car. I don't know if they were both tripping on acid that night or if it was just X, but he was super quiet. Ben kept making me touch the BB that was under the skin just below X's eye. It was like a party trick, except weirder, and apparently Ben made everyone do this. The story goes that X and another friend were dicking around years before, shooting BB guns at one another, and a BB got lodged in X's cheek, just under his eye.

When I transferred to Stone School, X was a student there as well. For a time, anyway. So were Ben, Rhiannon, and a bunch of other people. While most of us became inseparable, X and I bonded in a way I hadn't experienced before or since. He became like my brother, my other half. It was like he was half of my heart, the half that kept it beating, and if we were both walking around on the same planet everything would be ok. He was very protective of me and knew every one of my darkest secrets and fears. He was also a fucking thug.

X and a bunch of other friends ran the West Side of Ann Arbor. There were drugs, counterfeit money, street fights, and rivalries. I mean, you name it and it was probably happening. But X never wanted me to get mixed up in any of that garbage, so whenever shit was about to pop off while I was around he hug me and say, "Ok, I love you, sis, see you later."

I was 17 when X was arrested and charged with attempted murder. He pled guilty and in return the charge was reduced to assault with intent to do great bodily harm. There had been a street brawl at some big kegger in Ann Arbor. My friends had brought the keg tap and some frat brat randomly decided to start some shit. The kids who started the fight upped the ante by bringing baseball bats into it.

X was hit in the head and face with a bat and when I went to see him in the county jail it was hard to look at his face. At some point, the brawl spilled out into the street. A bunch of my friends made their way out of the melee and met up at a pizza place close by. After a moment, they realized one of them was missing and they had to go back and make sure he was all right. At that point, a keg was being dropped on some kid in the fight. The cops showed up and everyone scattered. In the midst of the chaos, the police focused on pursuing the small number of people they recognized because of their extensive criminal histories. One of them was X.

Because he took a plea bargain for lesser chargers, X spent a short time in prison and was then transferred to a boot camp which happened to be about ten miles from the home I shared with the evil stepbrothers in Chelsea. He spent ninety days in boot camp and was released with intensive parole for two years.

While he was locked up I wrote letters to him every single day, sometimes more than one. I would drive by daily and honk the horn, trying to catch them while they were out in the yard doing drills so that he'd know I was thinking of him. When he got out, my mom helped him get a job at the same store she worked at in downtown Ann Arbor. I have no fucking idea why she trusted me *or* him, but for whatever reason, she felt compelled to help keep him on the right track and out of trouble.

After all of this, X and I became even closer. He knew that I loved stars (and *why* I loved stars) and sometimes we would drive outside of the city to find a spot to park under the stars and fall asleep in the bed of my pickup truck. We were away from all of the noise of the city, but definitely not next to any corn fields because, as X so eloquently put it, "I've fucking seen 'Children of the Corn.'" That still makes me laugh.

It seemed fitting then, when laying out my sleeve, that I would get a sextant to honor my friendship with X. A sextant is a tool that pre-dated the compass; sailors used (and still use) sextants to map the stars and a ship's position at sea, especially in the worst of storm conditions. I always said X was my north star; he always guided me home.

So, knowing all of this, why wouldn't I use his actual name?

The last time that I spoke to X was around my birthday in August 2010. He had been living in California since late summer of 2007, but we still talked as regularly as possible and he came home for all of the important stuff like weddings and funerals. We had our annual birthday phone call and caught up for quite a while. I told him about the pregnancy and my plans to terminate. It was an emotional call, and he was there for me like always. Essentially, everything seemed normal.

Several days later I was having a *really* hard time with everything and just really wanted to hear his voice. I called his number and it went to straight to voicemail, but it wasn't his message on the voicemail anymore. It was just an automated robot-voicemail message. I thought maybe he'd changed his number for like the millionth time, so I reached out to his partner via Facebook messenger and just said, "Hey, can you let X know I need to talk to him and have him call me?"

I wasn't prepared for what came next. X's partner told me that days before, he had snapped. X had been drinking and doing hard drugs for a while and it didn't seem like a problem at first (spoiler alert: it's always a fucking problem, especially with addicts) but his behavior and moods were becoming more and more erratic. It culminated in an event just days before when X, drunk and high, terrorized his family.

His partner and two small children, I was told, spent the night cowering in a bedroom with a locked door and a cell phone in hand, waiting to call 911 if X forced his way into the room. When he eventually passed out on the floor in some part of the house, X's partner and the kids snuck out. Later, friends and family would help get as much of the family's worldly possessions as possible into a moving truck and help X's partner and kids essentially run away from him permanently, afraid of what might happen if he'd found them.

I was stunned, and I immediately reached out to X's mom to see how much of this I could believe. Her tears and exhaustion were palpable on the other end of the line and that told me most of what I needed to know. I'll never forget how she said, "You might be the only person who could get through to him now. We want to send him to rehab."

Unfortunately, she was wrong. X wouldn't answer my repeated phone calls or messages. After talking with X's mom I called our other sister, Rhiannon. This is what we always did — when there was a crisis, we called in the troops. I told Rhiannon everything I knew and told her that I hadn't been able to get X to answer any of my calls or messages, I was scared and didn't know what to do. Rhiannon called another friend, a recovering heroin addict, thinking that maybe *they* could get through to him.

In the middle of the night, I woke up to a series of text messages and voicemail messages from X. He told me that I'd sided with his enemy and the thief of his children and that it was unforgivable — that he never wanted to hear from me again, and if he heard of me speaking to anyone else about him that *he would kill me.*

I called him back and tried briefly to reason with him but there was no reasoning. He was dead fucking serious. We haven't communicated since, and I've never seen him again. I've stayed in touch with his parents and sister throughout the years, and get to keep up with his ex-partner and the kiddos via Facebook.

I don't regret the tattoo. You may find it surprising, but it's quite beautiful, really, and it matches my sister's butterfly. I miss X mostly every day and dream about him often. But I guess I grieved him like he was dead a long time ago, figuring the version of him that I knew really *was* dead. Sometimes there's no coming back from shit. This was one of those times. Sometimes it still feels like I'll stop breathing if he stops walking the earth, even if he did disown me the better part of a decade ago.

The Sewing Machine

I met Bradford in the sixth grade when my family moved from Flint to Chelsea. We were in classes together and somehow, he became my middle school boyfriend. Like a total dick, I broke up with him on Valentine's Day. When I left Chelsea schools for good I stopped seeing pretty much anyone I went to school with in Chelsea. It wasn't until I was in college, after Angela showed back up in my life, that I would see Bradford again.

Friendship is weird. Out of the billions of people on the planet, you meet certain other humans randomly and over time you become best friends and you can't imagine your life without them. My friendship with Brad was like that. I went from seeing him again for the first time to not being able to remember a time without him in my life, hardly noticing the transition. Brad came to all of my family parties with me and tried to help me keep my wild ass niece under control when she lived with me. We even had to keys to each other's apartments. More than once I had an asshole boyfriend tell me to choose between him and Brad. Y'all can guess how that went.

I don't know how many times Brad came through in an emergency for me, too many to count. Through all of the years of putting myself through college and then grad school, I had a lot of illness and health issues, mainly due to the toll stress took on my body.

I remember one time, in particular, calling Brad at about 3:00 am and telling him that I couldn't breathe right. My throat was so swollen it was hard even to talk. I had a high fever as well. He came over without hesitation and took me to the emergency room, practically carrying me to the car.

Brad sat with me and waited the whole time, and then took me to get my prescriptions, some popsicles, and other supplies at the all-night pharmacy. It turned out I had a double ear infection and upper-respiratory infection after traveling to London for a study abroad program, just weeks after my friends Mark and Dixon passed away. I guess it all just caught up to me.

Some of my greatest and most ridiculous antics are also some of my greatest memories with Brad. Like the night before my college graduation. We went to see my friends, Whitey Morgan & the 78s, play a show at a bar about 25 miles from home. It only took a couple of drinks for me to forget that I had to be up early the next day to walk in graduation, with my parents and grandparents in the audience, until I was wasted out of my gourd, finally remembering around midnight.

I was also supposed to have been the designated driver that night since I was supposed to walk at graduation the next day. Once I realized the error of my ways, Brad and I started slamming pitchers of cola in a (very failed) attempt to sober up. We ended up getting a ride from one of the band members and his wife, both friends of mine. Graduation was a rough day. I have wondered a time or two if I didn't sabotage myself because, subconsciously, I just didn't want to face that Mark wasn't there to walk with me.

I lost Brad for a couple of years in our early thirties over some dumb shit. His girlfriend at the time, now his wife, wasn't in the best space emotionally or psychologically when they were in the early stages of their relationship. I expressed concerns and flaked out on their wedding and it led to tension and bad blood. Brad and I would occasionally write letters back and forth to try and keep the connection and friendship a little bit alive, but it wasn't great.

Then, one night in 2011, after I'd just gone through *another* breakup with *another* drunk fuckstick, I'm standing in the frozen food aisle at Meijer, scouring the shelves for the perfect ice cream, when some lady comes charging straight at me with her shopping cart. I'm standing there, befuddled and half-ready to fight, when she gets close enough that I see it is none other than Brad's wife, Shannon.

At this point, I hadn't communicated with Brad in like a year and really thought I might never hear from him again. Shannon walks up with tears in her eyes, visibly shaken, and asks, "Can I hug you?" We hugged right there in that damn store, tears and all. We exchanged apologies and she told me that she'd been pushing Brad to reach out to me for quite some time but he'd been afraid it was too late.

When I got home from the grocery store that night I texted Brad something along the lines of, "I don't care how much time goes by or what happens, it's never too late." I think it was the very next day that I met up with Brad and Shannon to watch Shannon's daughter perform in her school play. From that day forward, it was like no time ever passed at all. Brad and Shannon had a son that I hadn't met, but you wouldn't have known it if you'd seen us all together days later. I became the extra family member, blended in without question.

I've had the idea in my head for years now that if I ever actually get married then Brad should be the one to walk me down the aisle. He really is like a brother to me. Brad is a quilter and has always gotten a lot of shit for it. I've always thought it was cool. At any rate, it made sense to me to add a small vintage sewing machine to my sleeve, to honor Brad and our friendship. It doesn't really go with the whole Navy/Sailor theme, but who gives a shit.

It's my body, and I get to make the rules.

Hold Fast and The Lighthouse

The last two pieces in my sleeve were more about me than anyone else. One is a ship's wheel with a banner that reads, "Hold fast," and the second is a lighthouse which filled in the last significant gaps. The ship's wheel was a message to me, at the age of 28, to stay on course, hold fast, and keep fucking going. I was finishing up grad school when it came time to add the piece. I'd survived some pretty tumultuous years and, in some cases, even thrived. I wasn't entirely sure where I was going. Hell, I *never* could have guessed I'd end up where I am now.

I said that the idea behind my sleeve was that it would represent the family members and friends who have been my beacons of light, guiding me back to myself and back home through life's storms. To me, that's what the lighthouse represents; it reminds me that all of those people are out there, contributing to who I am, to my story.

If ever I'm feeling lost and alone I've got a lifetime worth of memories I can walk through in my mind and be surrounded by the best parts of all of them again.

Tattoos featured:

Swallow, in memory of my dear friend Mark Kidd who KIA in Iraq in January, 2007. Completed in 2012.

The sextant, because X was my north star… until he wasn't anymore. Completed in 2009.

The sewing machine, in tribute to my best friend Brad. Completed in 2012.

CHAPTER NINE
The Story of Us

Life after the abortion

After the abortion, my heart was shattered, and the shame and guilt I felt were palpable. I was having frequent nightmares and would wake up crying. After I told them about terminating my pregnancy, my sister and brother-in-law paid for Brian and myself to visit Tennessee for a week to regroup and heal. It was one of the kindest things anyone has done for me. While there, I had a nightmare in which I heard a baby crying and when I finally found her, she turned to me and told me that she was supposed to be my daughter and asked why I didn't want her. I called my mother who talked me down from a panic attack.

The thing is, you can decide not to have a child, knowing that you're in no position to raise a child, and still struggle with the loss of that child. It might not make sense to anyone who hasn't experienced it or been forced to make such a choice, but I felt deep grief for what could have been. For *who* could have been. I love children. I've worked with children my entire adult life and spent my formative years helping raise other peoples' children. No way choosing to terminate a pregnancy wasn't going to impact me profoundly with a lot of mixed emotions.

Not long after my pregnancy, my niece turned up pregnant at the age of 19. This was the same niece that had lived with me years earlier, a situation that ended in catastrophe. When I learned that her relationship with the father of her baby was tenuous at best and violent at worst, I felt compelled to help, especially when the physical conflict between them was taking place even after my great-niece was born. Brian encouraged me to invite the girls to live with me, in my apartment in Ypsilanti. We both wanted to help; I think we were both trying to fill a hole in our hearts that neither one of us wanted to admit existed.

It was a frigid night in late October when my niece and I were texting back and forth. She decided she wanted to come to Michigan with the baby to get out of Florida and away from the father. The family quickly planned – my sister and brother-in-law in Tennessee would drive to Florida and collect the girls, and then I'd drive down from Michigan to Tennessee to pick them up and bring them the rest of the way home.

Logistically and financially it wasn't easy. I was in the middle of midterms and had a long paper to write over the same weekend we planned for the trip. I drove a 1991 Oldsmobile Ninety-Eight that was not likely to get there and back safely, so I had to rent a car to make the trek. Except, my first paycheck from my new job running a community center was four days late. I had to call my boss and essentially ask for emergency financial assistance.

Cindil decided to play hooky and called out from work to drive down with me. She was sick, it turned out, but I don't know how I would have gotten through the trip without her. There was a massive snowstorm that struck in Indiana and made driving a challenge. We decided to stop for the night and not take any unnecessary chances. I wrote my midterm late into the night by the glow of my laptop screen in a hotel attached to a Waffle House just outside of Indianapolis. We finished the rest of the drive the next day, lacking sleep.

You can't always fix what's broken.

For the first couple of months, having the girls at home was incredible. Brian and I didn't live together, but he began to spend more and more time at my place, spending whole weekends with us quite regularly. He lived about an hour away from Ypsilanti, in Jackson, and as he became more involved in helping to care for the baby and such, it made less sense for him to drive back and forth each day.

Brian and I both loved that baby girl to the moon. When

she would wake up for a bottle or a diaper change late at night, we would sometimes race to see who could get to the crib first. Brian would often dance with her and sing old Johnny Paycheck or Waylon Jennings songs to her to calm her when she was fussy. He even made sure to be there for her first Christmas, driving out late on Christmas Eve, surprising us, and hanging out for Christmas morning to watch us help her open all of her presents. His deep love for the girls made me love him even more.

Unfortunately, as had happened when my niece lived with me years before, things started to turn south. She was young and immature, caught up in the sensationalism of having an ex-boyfriend in Florida and the baby in Michigan. She spent most of her waking hours caught up in melodrama on Facebook. I was not in any position to process or deal with the madness.

Looking back, I recognize that I was having a PTSD relapse as a result of the abortion and was also in a full-blown decline of my Major Depressive Disorder. In addition to the complicated living situation, I was working a full-time job that was very demanding, both emotionally and intellectually, as well as physically draining. I was also finishing up the final two semesters of my graduate school coursework. It was all too much for me. I had very little patience and very little emotional control.

The boundaries set when my niece moved in with me included that she either needed to be working full time or going to school full time by April 2012. I would assist with childcare, but she would have to do her best to schedule her classes or work shifts around my schedule since I generally worked day-time hours and had classes at night. She would need to be contributing to the household through wages earned or financial assistance provided as a student because I only made about $900 a month and had used the last of *my* financial aid to pay for rent up front for six months when the girls moved in.

As April grew nearer, my niece's behavior became increasingly erratic. Plans kept changing and nothing she said made sense. Later I'd learn that that was because, unbeknownst to me, she had been planning for some time to take the baby back to Florida and move back in with the baby's father and his parents. I got a phone call from another family member who filled me in on her plans to return to Florida. The same family member informed me that I was being portrayed as being abusive toward my niece and the baby, threatening to kick them out and throw all their belongings in the dumpster.

I was devastated.

Shattered.

It was the straw that broke the very fragile camel's back.

I drove home from work that night, stormed into the apartment, and told my niece to pack up everything she could of her and the baby's and load it into the car because I was taking her to her mother's house. (Her mother, my oldest sister, lived about an hour and a half away in Lansing.) It was the only thing I could think to do. This only further complicated things with the entire family because, at that point, I had estranged from my oldest sister, and she was dealing with a load of child custody related drama herself of which I was entirely unaware.

Driving to Lansing that night I asked my niece why she'd done it. Why had she strung me along, using me for all that I was worth, knowing full well that she didn't intend to live up to her end of the bargain, and saying such awful things about me to our family? She paused and responded with perceptible vitriol, "Because I could."

When we arrived in Lansing, my sister and her partner helped my niece unload all of their things from the car, and they all went inside. Not a word was spoken to or around me. No questions asked. They took the baby inside, and I didn't see or talk to my sister or my niece again for six years.

When it all falls down

To say that I fell apart after the girls were gone would be an understatement. The apartment felt lonely and vacant. No more baby giggles or cries, no more chatting with my niece over trashy reality TV, no more Brian dancing and singing to the baby in the evenings. I felt alone in a way that was deeper and more devastating than I ever could have imagined. I cried constantly and had suicidal ideations and panic attacks daily. It was everything I could do to drag myself out of bed every day.

At the time, I was the Director of a community center in a public housing project, and my kids and families there counted on me to show up every day and be there to help with homework, cook dinner, advocate for them with the Department of Human Services or the Public Housing Commission, and so on. So, not getting out of bed was not conducive to keeping my job. Meager as the income may have been, it was better than nothing.

One night, when Brian was over after the girls had gone, he said to me, "All of the stray humans you keep bringing into your life keep turning on you… maybe it's time you try for a dog?" I'd wanted a dog for months and had even visited the local shelter one weekend to see a three-legged dog named Walter. He was being adopted into a family with a little girl who loved him the second she laid eyes on him, and I told myself I wasn't meant to have a dog. How the hell would I afford a dog? How the hell would I care for the dog when I could hardly care for myself? Also, what about my long days away at work and school? No, a dog was unreasonable. I resigned myself to continue with the empty-feeling apartment. And heart.

While working at the community center, I always tried to instill in my kids there that it was important to serve one's community, especially since their community did a lot to help them. They lived in subsidized housing, got Christmas gifts from volunteers and donors each year, had backpacks and school supplies collected and donated every school year, and other things of this nature. I started to work on finding ways in which they could give back.

Some of the kids were pretty terrible at interacting with animals and treating them respectfully. Many of them lacked any experience around animals, especially dogs, and those that did have experience being around animals hadn't necessarily been taught how to treat them with compassion. Hell, a lot of the kids I worked with were treated worse at home than you can imagine. Why would they have more respect for animals than they did themselves? Especially when self-respect was in such short supply for many of them.

I decided one day that I would take them to the Humane Society of Huron Valley, in Ann Arbor, to take a class to learn about cats and dogs, spaying and neutering animals, and properly caring for or treating pets. It had more of an impact than I anticipated. As we left that day, one of the boys I worked with asked, "Kelly, could we come back here sometime and help take care of the animals and give back to our community that way?"

"Yes, absolutely we can," I replied. And we did.

It was a Saturday morning in May 2012 when we were scheduled to volunteer at the Humane Society. Myself and one other Director (from a different community center that was run by the same organization) were set to take something like twenty kids and teens to volunteer. We would spend the morning cleaning up the walking trails and grounds around the shelter. The mission was to keep the trails and grounds as safe as possible for dog-walking and play time.

After two hours of intense and laborious cleanup work, the volunteer manager came outside to tell us that the volunteers who had been walking the dogs around the trails that day were all coming in to brag on how good the kids were doing outside. As a reward for their hard work, she invited us all inside to meet the dogs in the shelter and hand out some treats and pets. The kids enthusiastically accepted the invitation.

As we made the rounds through the kennels, I spotted her. *The dog*. She was a white boxer with one blue eye and one brown eye and the saddest, most precious face I'd ever seen. A volunteer quickly walked up to caution me that the dog was deaf, so I needed to be careful and not move too quickly. I slowly eased my hand into the kennel through the bars, and she placed her paw in my hand and looked into my eyes like she was reading my soul. I almost cried.

I quickly snapped a photo of her and sent it via text message to both my best friend Cindil and Brian, the boyfriend. The kids noticed me spending time by her kennel and all gathered around me, encouraging me to take her home. I told them that of course, that I couldn't. It wasn't practical, and we needed to get going and get back to the community center as their parents were expecting them home soon.

For a week I couldn't stop thinking about "Luna." (That was the name she had been assigned at the shelter.) Brian and I even casually started doing research on white boxers and working with deaf dogs. Still, I tried to tell myself that it was impossible and ridiculous and that she simply couldn't come home with me.

But then one night, Brian told me that my sister in Tennessee had sent him a couple of hundred dollars and told him to do something nice for me. She had been worried about me and how depressed I'd been since the girls had left in April. He'd been trying to decide what to do with the money, whether to take me away for a weekend or something else, and he asked, "Do you want to go get your dog?"

I immediately checked the Human Society website, and she was still listed as being in the shelter. In a delightful twist of fate, I learned that the shelter was over-crowded and overcapacity, so all dogs over seven months old were discounted to a 50% adoption fee of $75. They were all being sent home with a basket of toys and things, and a bag of dog food as well. Luna was eight months old. That settled it. We left the apartment immediately and headed for the shelter.

Formerly Luna, now Rosebud

We weren't the only people who had come to visit Luna that day. When we first arrived at the shelter, one of the staff members spotted me and said, "There's another family thinking of adopting her, but we don't feel they're right for her. Hurry and get back there!" We got our kennel visitor's pass and waited at her kennel for a volunteer to come and let her out.

We went out to the large playpen outside, and when they brought Luna in and let her off leash to play with us, she ran her face off. She zoomed around in circles and played Juke and Jive like an NFL pro. I was laughing hysterically. She was quick to hand out kisses as well. The volunteers and I agreed – she and I were meant for each other.

When we went inside to complete the adoption papers, they gave us Luna's history as they knew it. She had been with a family previously, but her person had died, and she had somehow run off. Being a deaf dog means that when you run off, it's incredibly difficult to be recalled and you can get lost very easily. She'd been found by someone jogging in the woods around Ann Arbor, and brought to the shelter.

She had a mass on her leg upon arrival that had been surgically removed and tested negative for cancer. She was spayed and received all her vaccinations, and eventually, her person's wife showed up at the shelter to retrieve her. She hadn't been willing to reimburse the shelter for the medical costs or pay an adoption fee, though, and the staff said they didn't feel good about sending Luna home with her. So, at the shelter, she stayed, until I showed up. She knew a few signed commands like, "come," and "good girl." She came home with me, discount pricing and all. It was the day before Mother's Day.

When we got back to my apartment that afternoon, we began

to discuss names for the new addition. Luna didn't feel right, and Cindil had a dog named Lena, so it seemed far too cheesy for two best friends to have matchy-matchy dog names. Brian looked down at her at one point and said, "She needs a good honky-tonk name. She looks like a rose. Like a rambling rose." Just then, the story of her first person dying popped into my head and I could hear Johnny Cash singing, "Give My Love to Rose" in my head. So, Luna became Rosebud, who eventually became Rosebud Marie Eleanor Frances Mendenhall.

What did I get myself into?

Rosebud and I bonded fiercely in no time at all. She became my reason to get up and leave bed every day. It wasn't for my job, my family or friends, or my relationship with Brian. He actually ghosted out on me not long after Rosebud came home. He disappeared from my life altogether, stopped answering phone calls or text messages. It would be eight months before I heard from him again. I sometimes wonder if Brian didn't know that he planned on this disappearing act and that this is why he suggested I get the dog. I'll never know the answer to that.

Except for my mom, sister Sara, and best friend Cindil, no one around me knew just how dark things were for me at this time. I went to a doctor's appointment not long after adopting Rosebud and bringing her home. This doctor had been my doctor since age 19, so she was familiar with my depressive cycles and anxiety disorders. During this period, I had been sick often and was subsequently with some illnesses related to stress. When I went for my regular check-in with the doctor, she asked me if I was getting any physical exercise to help with my anxiety and depression.

I lit up like a Christmas tree as I enthusiastically told her all about the new addition to my home. I told her that I was walking Rosebud every morning before work, how I would take her to local parks with tennis courts so that she could run around off-leash and chase tennis balls. I also explained that she often accompanied me to work and that the kids at the community center and I would take her for long walks together. My doctor listened intently, remarked that she hadn't seen me this happy in quite some time, and said, "You know what, Kelly? I think this dog is what's saving you. She brought you back to life."

What I know better than most anything else in my life is that Rosebud was the piece of my heart that I didn't realize was missing. She made the world less scary and easier to tolerate. She made coming home an utter joy, whereas the months just before her adoption had felt so empty and lonesome, so utterly meaningless. The snuggles Rosebud gives are top notch and can't be beat. Because she's deaf, she gets just as much comfort from touching me as I was getting (and still get) from having physical contact with her. This is especially true at night when I am attempting to sleep, as that is my brain's favorite time to send me into anxiety spirals and full-blown panic attacks.

If you know as much about Boxers as a breed as I did when I adopted Rosebud, then you know approximately 5% of what you need to know to prepare for having a Boxer at home. They're often referred to as the Peter Pan breed because they never grow up. They're almost always as goofy and playful into adulthood as they are as puppies. Boxers, and especially deaf boxers, are prone to pretty severe separation anxiety. Beyond that, Boxers are susceptible to a myriad of health issues. And Rosebud is no exception to any of these. But my neuroses and her neuroses seemed to make us fit together just perfectly, like two jigsaw pieces in the fabric of the universe who spent an immeasurable amount of time waiting to find one another.

It is common for Boxers to get cancer, have respiratory issues, be blind or deaf (or both if they are white), and have neurological and heart conditions. Rosebud has had a little of everything over the years. During her first year home, it was chronic cases of kennel cough, bronchitis, and pneumonia. In her second year home, she had what we now know was her first seizure. At the time that it happened, the doctors thought that she had a syncopal event and that her heart may have stopped momentarily – I had to take her to Michigan State University to see a dog cardiologist and everything.

In the years since, Rosebud has survived emergency bladder stone surgery – this was in 2013, when her urethra was 100% blocked by the stones and she was in danger of dying-threatening kidney failure; dog flu that nearly killed her in 2014; a cancer scare and surgery in 2015; two different injuries to both eyeballs in 2016, both of which almost rendered her blind in each eye; and another operation in September of 2018 for what turned out this time to be an actual mast cell (cancer) tumor. I've had not one, but *two* online fundraisers to help raise money to save Rosebud's life. People were overwhelmingly supportive in both instances.

The love terrorist

Through all of this…through all the scariness and pain and illness, I'll be damned if Rosebud doesn't remain the happiest, goofiest, most tenacious, stubborn, precious, and crazy-making creature on four legs that anyone could ever hope to encounter. She steals entire sticks of butter and loaves of bread, once got a dozen farm-fresh eggs off the counter and decorated the house with them and has even taken raw cookie dough waiting to go into the oven off baking sheets on the kitchen counter. She also once swiped half a cheeseball off a table of food at her aunt Cindil's.

She loves with 110% of her heart, all day, every day. I've never seen a dog get so attached to anyone she identifies as her people. When we all still lived in Ypsilanti and could be together nearly every day, Rosebud would almost dislocate my shoulder trying to run after her aunt Cindil every time Cindil left our apartment. She can go one, two, even as much as three years without seeing family, friends, and loved ones from back in Michigan and she'll still nearly do backflips of joy upon seeing them again. I don't care what anyone says about the memories of dogs, or animals in general. *This* dog never forgets someone she loves.

At some point years ago, my friend Lisa nick-named Rosebud the Love Terrorist, because of how she literally cannot contain herself with excitement and elation at the sight of someone she loves. She will stomp on all of your vital organs, lick your face raw, jump up and down to greet you, and knows nothing about personal space – she's been known to sit on my head while I attempt to do my back and leg stretches on the yoga mat.

Rosebud doesn't know how to love any less than that; she's just not wired that way. She's kind of like me that way, and that's why eventually my friends and I realized I'm a love terrorist, too. This dog makes me laugh out loud every single day. Even now, as I've been in chronic pain for nearly two years and living the majority of my life on the couch. On the worst days, the darkest and saddest days, 7.5 years after she first came home, she's still here giving me a reason to get out of bed every day. I can never thank her enough. I may have paid an adoption fee on that day in May 2011, but that was the day that Rosebud rescued me. She's been saving me one day at a time, ever since.

Part of the process of writing this book was that I had professional photographs taken. I needed headshots and an author bio picture, but I also needed to shoot photos of the tattoos themselves. I sent a group of pictures from the shoot out in a group text to some family members and also shared them with friends. The next day I got a text message that read something along the lines of, "Your photos turned out beautifully, but I'd like to know why your left arm is so much emptier than your right arm." I explained that it had been more than two years since my last tattoo, having been out of work for more than a year and a half because of chronic pain and health issues. I didn't know when I would be able to afford another.

The person responded by asking if there were tattoos that I knew I wanted to get but didn't have the money for. I think I listed about ten ideas on my tattoo wish-list. Then I got another message, "I'm going to send you a check, and I'd like for you to use it to get one of those tattoos on your wish-list and start filling up that arm." I couldn't believe it. For me, a person who expresses so much of herself through her tattoos and also uses getting tattooed as a form of stress relief, this was one hell of a gift.

When the check arrived, I messaged Jason, the artist who had done my Nerdzilla piece, and told him that I had $125 and needed a new tattoo. I said that maybe we should do something related to the concept of being a love terrorist. We made plans for me to come in and get the piece done later that same week, on a Friday. He sent me a sketch the day before my appointment.

It was a whimsical rendering of Rosebud's face, with the word "Love" above her head, and the word "Terrorist" below.

I cried.

We moved forward with the concept.

The next day, as we were finishing my appointment, I got a call from Rosebud's veterinarian. He was calling to deliver biopsy results. He told me that while the mass we had removed from Rosebud's back weeks earlier was, in fact, a mast cell tumor, that the pathologist believed that the surgery had been curative and she was going to be just fine.

The day that I met Rosebud in May 2011.

The sketch I received from Jason for the concept of the love terrorist tattoo.

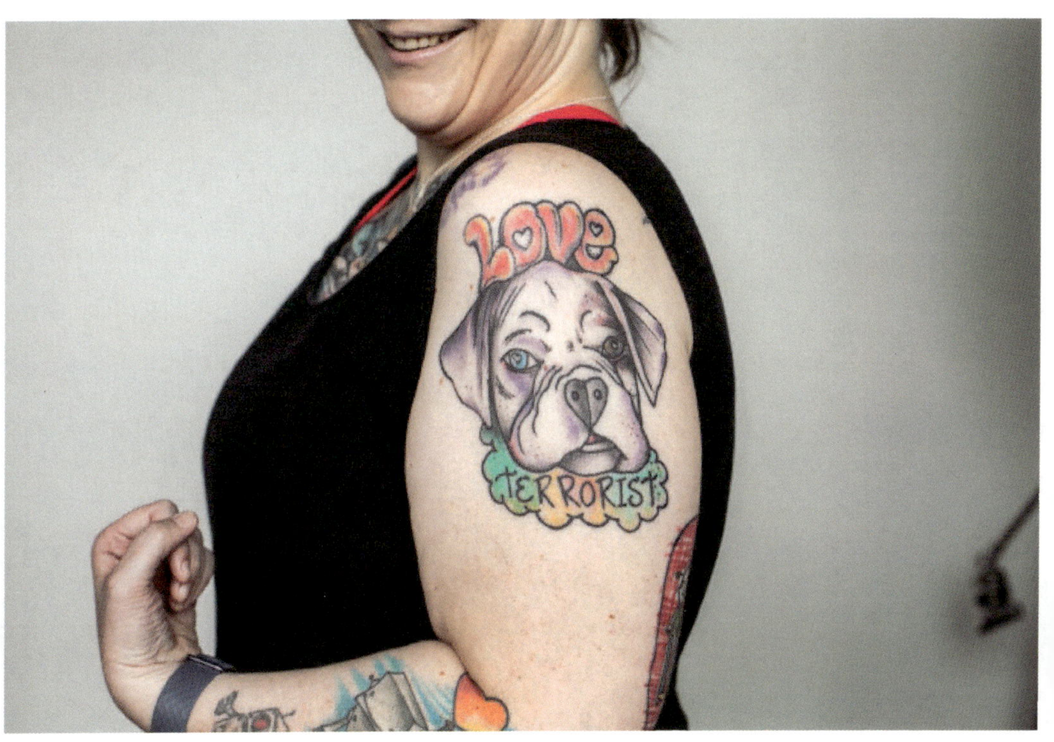

Tattoo designed and completed by Jason MacDonald of Electric Hand Tattoo Company in Nashville, Tennessee. Age at the time of completion, 36.

CHAPTER TEN

Nerdzilla, Part 1

My friend Shane

I made friends with Shane thanks to the Inked Nation website, the now-forgotten social networking site for people in the tattoo and body modification industries and subcultures. It's been more than a decade now since Shane and I became friends. I can't remember exactly how we connected or why, but our friendship grew organically and rapidly from the very first moment we came into contact. And while I lack memory about the specifics that brought us together, I do remember that one of the first things I learned about him was that he was a pro wrestler.

Shane "Riot" DeCambra is the third-generation in his family to spend time in the world of professional wrestling. Shane has always wrestled as Riot, and for many years rocked one of the tallest liberty-spike mohawks I've ever seen. His father, Rex Farmer, wrestles as Shane Kody, and his Grandfather, Woody Farmer, was a wrestling pioneer who started his own wrestling school after joining the sport in the 1960s[1]. To my knowledge, they were the only three-generation wrestling family in the game, and sadly that came to be just two generations after Shane's grandfather died several years back.

I *loved* wrestling as a kid. Hulk Hogan was one of my heroes. I was eight years old when my mom scored tickets to see the World Wrestling Federation Summer Slam (1990) at the IMA Sports

---

[1]http://slam.canoe.com/Slam/Wrestling/2007/03/20/3790664.html

Arena in Flint, Michigan. Hulk Hogan vs. The Earthquake was the main event and I lost my ever-loving mind when Hulk Hogan made his way to the ring that day. It's honestly one of the best memories of my childhood; I'm not ashamed to say that I desperately wanted one of those rip-away Hulk Hogan t-shirts. Alas, we couldn't afford one.

When Shane told me that he was a wrestler and shared the history of his family in the sport, I shared this experience with him. He responded by sharing a photograph of him and Hulk Hogan when Shane was a little kid, probably younger than I was when I got to see Hulk Hogan wrestle live.

Have you seen the movie *Step Brothers*, with Will Ferrell and John C. Riley? There's a moment in which, after spending most of the movie fighting, nearly to the death, they realize how much they have in common, and Will Ferrell's character exclaims, "Did we just become best friends?!" to which John C. Reily's character responds, simply, "Yup!" That's about how I felt about Shane when that photo of him and Hulk Hogan popped up on my computer screen.

A love for wrestling isn't the only shared characteristic that runs in Shane's family, though. Big, soft hearts also appear to be an innate trait. Shane is one of the most loving and sensitive men I know, no matter how he may try to conceal it with a tough and menacing outward persona. He loves *hard*, which means heartbreak and betrayal rip him apart just as much as love, laughter, and compassion hold him together. Shane and I also share those characteristics.

The worst job ever

I'd graduated with my Bachelor's in Political Science in April 2007 and worked the world's most humiliating and physically taxing job. Ok, maybe not *the world*'s most, but it was *my* most humiliating and physically taxing job. I was a patient transporter at St. Joseph Mercy Hospital in Ann Arbor. As a patient transporter, I walked an average of 12 or 13 miles a day, roaming the halls of the hospital, taking patients from their room to procedure or imaging centers, and back.

Non-ambulatory patients were the worst because chances were, you were going to screw your back up somehow trying to move them from their bed to the stretcher. Nurses would run and hide like cockroaches when they heard a transporter coming down the patient room hallways with a stretcher. This was especially common when the patient was non-ambulatory, elderly, or an otherwise general pain-in-the-ass.

The job was awful. They timed you on how long it took you to get a patient from point A to point B and you had to stop and log in all the details of your trip into computers sprinkled throughout the hospital. That left very little room for actually being nice to patients, and I wasn't built for that shit.

I remember one incident, I had an elderly man I had to take from his room down for a CT scan. He had dementia and kept asking the same questions over and over. He couldn't remember if he was hungry or not because he couldn't remember if he had eaten anything. Something about him really broke my heart — I had a deep sense of empathy for the torture I imagined it must be to literally lose your mind. No matter what I've faced or had to survive in life, I've had a pretty good, strong mind. The idea of losing that and not remembering myself or my surroundings from one moment to the next was, and is, utterly terrifying.

When we were heading back to his room, he told me that he thought he was hungry, but I knew that dining services had been closed for hours, it was about 9:00 pm. I decided to say screw the damn time-clocks and fix him a snack.

I got the man settled into bed, rewound, and pushed play on the video cassette in the TV they'd set up in his room for him. When I said, "Oh, A Streetcar Named Desire! This is a good one!" his eyes lit up and he smiled as he questioned how on Earth I would know that, being as young as I was. I told him the story about watching it in a literature class in high school, how handsome I thought Marlon Brando was, and how before I'd seen "Streetcar," I'd only ever known Marlon Brando as the old, fat, Godfather.

Once he was comfortable and watching his movie I went and found supplies in the nurse's station kitchen to make him a turkey sandwich. Honestly, making him that sandwich and offering him that little bit of comfort was one of only a handful of times I felt like I was worth a single shit at that job.

I was able to make him so happy and provide him such comfort when he'd been so scared and alone when I first picked him up. It only took an extra five minutes. I let the dispatcher know I was done with the run and heading back and she made a comment about how I'd taken so long. I said if they wanted to write me up for taking better care of a patient they could do it, I didn't give a shit. And I meant it.

I developed a strong rapport with a lot of the patients I transported, especially WWII vets. They got a real kick out of my tattoos and hearing the stories behind them. I had fewer back then, but my robots and the cartoon with the fallen star were visible to them. One gentleman, as we pulled into the procedure wing where he was to undergo his next test, turned to me and said, "I haven't thought about my pain in twenty minutes. Thank you for telling me those stories. Nothing else has helped me forget about my pain."

It was this job that I lost because of the stress and illness caused by my relationship with the abusive tattoo artist ex-boyfriend. When I got back from the trip to Wisconsin in early 2008, reality hit. After graduating from college in 2007, and while hunting for my first post-degree job, I'd been mostly living on credit cards. I got the job as a patient transporter and less than six months later I'd lost it, which left me in even more of a lurch. The creditors were calling and harassing me, and I needed to figure out what the hell to do with my life pretty quickly.

School has always been sort of an escape for me. So long as I was in school and keeping myself excessively busy, I didn't have time to let too much else get to me. I did better at surviving my stepbrothers when I had school as a safe haven. I'd done well at putting off my grief for two of my best friends who died during my senior year of undergrad by immersing myself in the final semester and taking on as much work for the staff and faculty in the Political Science department as I could. Add raising a teenager and two young boys, plus taking a study-abroad class in England to the mix. I was good at avoidance. It was always when I was *out* of school that shit hit the fan.

Logically, I decided it was time to go to graduate school. I'd planned on it anyway but hadn't really thought about when. Financial destitution and a stark lack of direction seemed as good a reason as any to go ahead and start right then. At least I'd have financial aid to help keep me afloat. I applied for graduate school that spring and was accepted to start in the summer semester of 2008. Ready or not, here I came.

Nerdzilla was born

It was early 2008 when Shane and I sparked our friendship and it wasn't long after the job loss and break up with the abusive ex that we began to become quite close. We were in touch mostly online, occasionally via text or phone call; sometimes there would be weeks in-between talks and sometimes we'd talk every fucking day. It just depended on what kind of shit we were trying to trudge through at the time. So, in late summer of 2008, when we were on the phone and I mentioned something about classes starting soon and having just moved into a new place with a new roommate, Shane stopped the conversation dead in its tracks. "What do you mean, *classes*? I thought you just got done with those?!" he exclaimed.

I responded, "Well, yeah, but that was last year. I graduated with my Bachelor's degree. Now, I'm going for my Master's."

He said, "That's it. You're the biggest nerd I know. From now on I'm calling you Nerdzilla".

And he did.

And does.

The ill-fated Vermont relationship

I met another man on Inked Nation, in 2008, named Adrian. Within one or two conversations we were talking every night. Sometimes *all* night, until the sun came up. It was always by phone or video chat. In 2009, I traveled from Michigan to Vermont twice to visit him and his daughter(s) before moving there in December 2009 to try and make a go of a relationship with both of us in the same place.

I never even really got to unpack in Vermont because there was no space for me—in both a figurative and very literal sense. Adrian was a hoarder and the house was in utter chaos when I arrived. The snowstorms that dumped six-plus feet of snow on us shortly after my arrival didn't help. It's hard to get things, trash, and clutter out of a house when even the people are trapped inside.

The entire story isn't just mine to tell, but it was over even more quickly than it began. I drove out of Vermont on February 14, 2010. I was not in good shape emotionally. Deciding to leave Adrian and his girls was one of the hardest and most necessary decisions of my life. He wasn't healthy enough to sustain a relationship with himself, let alone anyone else, and I was too healthy to allow him to drag me down. He was a shell of a man. But it took me being there, up close and personal, for me to see that.

I live with Generalized Anxiety Disorder (GAD), Post Traumatic Stress Disorder (PTSD), and Major Depressive Disorder (MDD).

I'm petrified of bridges and was in the throes of deep heartache and sorrow. You can imagine, then, that I was not in the best shape for driving back across the country from Vermont in the middle of winter.

I wasn't sure what the fuck I was going to do beyond getting back to my parents' house and setting up shop temporarily while I figured out what to do next. Coincidentally, Shane was having his own emotional crisis at this time, also due to heartbreak, and he was also a hot fucking mess. He called me at some point early on in my drive back, having no clue what I was going through until he called. We kept each other company through the heartache and confusion for a good bit.

I remember getting to a hotel, somewhere in New York, only a few hours from whence I'd come and taking some Ativan to help calm my nerves and get me to sleep. I fell asleep with the phone in my hand, talking with Shane.

Three things got me through that road trip — Shane, *Bridget Jones's Diary* on Audiobook and Michal J. Fox's reading of his book, *Always Looking Up: The adventures of an incurable optimist*.

How people ever got through anxiety- and heartbreak-ridden road trips before audiobooks, iPods, and cell phones, I have no idea. The trip shouldn't have taken more than two days, the route I was on was something like a 14-hour drive. But being as fragile as I was, I did everything I could to avoid large bridges and snow storms, neither of which are easy to dodge when driving through New York or the mountains of Pennsylvania in February.

Nerdzilla rebuilds

I've had many nicknames in my life. Crayola was the nickname I got between 8th and 9th grade because I changed the color of my hair so often. Just after college, my friend Aaron started calling me Klutzbot, out of the combination of my love for robots and the fact that I am one of the klutziest people on the planet. My mom and Aunt Judy have called me Kell-Bell for as long as I can remember, and at some point, my dear friend Bradford picked up on it and still uses it consistently. But Nerdzilla sort of took on a life of its own.

At some point, kind of as a joke, I changed my Facebook profile name from Kelly Mendenhall to Kelly Nerdzilla Mendenhall like six or seven years ago. It stuck and that's how people came to know and think of me. I took a sort of pride in the name Nerdzilla. I was the first person in my family (and still the only, I believe) to earn a Master's Degree. I've always loved words, written and oral storytelling, and learning.

I found safety and solace in my imagination when I was reading, and clarity and enlightenment when I was writing – especially in my late teens and early twenties. But I never could have predicted, not in a million years, what the name Nerdzilla and my life *with* that name would become.

Nerdzilla tattoo sketch

CHAPTER ELEVEN

Nerdzilla, Part 2

For all the dreams I've dreamed before...

When I started college, I wanted to change the world. That might sound idealistic, and even my 36-year-old self rolls her eyes just slightly at my 21-year-old self. I was going to change the world. I had no idea how I was going to change the world, but I was fire-under-my-ass determined that I would do it. I would leave the world a better place than I found it. There wasn't a damn thing life could throw at me that would stop me. (Trust me, life tried.)

With that grit and determination, I got my Associates in Secondary Education, because, I thought, "Teachers! Teachers change the world! I'll do that. I'll focus on English Language and Literature, and I'll write a best-selling book someday while also being a teacher because writers can change the world too if people are paying attention to what they're saying!"

Alas, I didn't do that. Well, not the teaching part. I decided I would get perpetually fired for saying things like, "Christopher Columbus was an asshole with a bad sense of direction." So, I settled on my Bachelor's in Political Science. I thought, "I'll infiltrate the system and blast Dead Kennedys in the halls of the White House when I meet with some future president about how I'm changing the world!"

Well, that hasn't happened either. I'm sure *someone* has blasted Dead Kennedys in the halls of White House or Congress, but it hasn't been me. In the end, I got a Master's in Public Administration with certifications in Nonprofit Management and Public Personnel Management.

Finally, I thought, "*YES*! I'll work in nonprofit and fill the gap between what the public needs and what the private and public sectors can give to the public! That's how I'll change the world!"

I would do good for the world and do well for myself.

Rise up and come up.

Simple plan, yes?

I believe I actually said, out loud on several occasions, "I will change this fucking world for the better if it kills me!"

And it almost has.

I entered the nonprofit sector, officially, around 2008.

What am I even doing with my life?

At the time that I graduated with my Master's in Public Administration in April 2012, I was running a community center in a public housing project. I was overseeing all of the services within that center, such as an emergency food pantry and community meal program, the after-school program and extracurricular activities for children and youth, and also serving as an advocate for adult residents. Being the Director of the community center was one of the best and worst jobs that I've ever had.

It was the best because I was on the ground floor of advocacy and making an impact in the community in which I served. I loved spending time with the kids each day after school, and sometimes on the weekends or during summer programs. The job made me feel like I was really *doing* something. It was the worst because it was emotionally taxing. I dealt with shootings, domestic violence incidents, 24/7 phone calls from residents, calls to Child Protective Services (CPS) for abuse and neglect, and a boss who was the very definition of evil and manipulative. (In all likelihood, she probably *is* a sociopath. A real joy to work for.)

I had been with that organization for nearly three years when my position was eliminated, and the sociopathic boss attempted to bribe me into keeping my mouth shut about the dirt I'd seen done there. For example, there were times when she'd asked me to lie on grant reports for local government offices, or make up numbers for people served because, as she said, "No one from [the city] was ever going to check anyhow."

Or, she'd try to force staff to withhold programs and services from residents unless they participated in a program we wanted them to or signed some paper or completed some survey about our services. This was a clear violation of the National Association of Social Workers Code of Ethics, not to mention just some really grimy shit to do to poor people.

The worst of what I witnessed was when she would try to persuade staff from the Public Housing Authority to create excuses to enter a resident's home without their knowledge or permission. She'd suggest that they should do so under the guise of a water leak or some other emergency, and try to find drugs or drug paraphernalia in the home. The motivation for this was so that she could then persuade the Housing Commission to evict them because she didn't want to have to deal with them as clients anymore.

My boss and I had been locked in a battle for over a year, me pushing back on these issues and her trying to bully me into doing her bidding. Finally, on a Friday afternoon in April 2013, she showed up with a Board member I'd never seen before and unceremoniously let me go.

She offered me six months' worth of salary and continued health benefits if I agreed to sign away my rights to tell anyone about anything I'd seen or heard while I was employed there; anything related to the organization, *from the beginning of time.* I'm not kidding, that phrase, "From the beginning of time," was in the actual Non-Disclosure Agreement. (I still have it, for the sake of a laugh now and then.)

I told her to go fuck herself and went directly from the meeting to my lawyer's office. Try as we did to expose what she was doing, the President of the Board chose not to take any action when a signed affidavit and account of my experiences in the organization was delivered in the summer of 2013. At least when it was all said and done, I could still sleep at night.

Months later I was offered what I thought was my dream job for an organization in Nashville. I was hired for the position of Director of Development for a brand-new organization that used music to form connections and inspire healing for PTSD and other mental health conditions, stop bullying in public schools, and aid the rehabilitation of inmates in local jails and prisons. I accepted the position in June 2013, just two months shy of my 31st birthday. I thought all of my dreams were coming true. I found and rented an apartment online, sight unseen. My mom and I pooled resources to rent a U-Haul, and off I went. I arrived in Nashville on July 23, 2013.

Just a couple of weeks into working full-time at my dream

job, developing program budgets and writing funding proposals, I was laid off. They'd lost their founding donor; there was no money to pay me. Everything fell apart.

I seriously contemplated tucking tail and running back to Michigan where everything was familiar and safe, but I didn't. Instead, I took a job at a Staples to be doing *something* while I sought full-time work in my field. Nothing humbles a person quite like hanging their MPA on the wall (next to various other degrees and certificates of achievement) only to end up working at Staples a short year later, wearing a fucking elf hat on Black Friday and making $7 an hour. And receiving food stamps. It sucked.

In February 2014 I landed a job as the Grants Manager and Development Coordinator for a large Christian organization in Downtown Nashville. Huzzah! I was incredibly excited to finally put my very specialized set of skills to good use, and I did. However, just after New Year's in 2015, at the staff holiday luncheon, I'd witnessed a conversation in which the Executive Director said that all Muslims should be rounded up and shot. Just wipe them all out. You know, in the name of Christ. Those weren't comments or philosophies that I could tolerate, and I knew I would have to get out as quickly as possible. Things felt even uglier when SCOTUS legalized same-sex marriage, and I found myself missing my friends' wedding because I feared being caught on camera and losing my job because of it.

In August 2015 I ran as fast as I could away from the degradation and humiliation inflicted upon me at that organization. Thinking that maybe front lines work or administrative work in disorganized-and-insane grassroots organizations just wasn't meant for me, I decided to make a change. August 31, 2015, was my first day as a Foster Parent Recruiter and Trainer with a large organization based in middle Tennessee. With over 2,000 employees and entire departments dedicated to research and policy, I thought, "Surely, I can avoid the pitfalls of the organizations I've worked for in the past."

Unfortunately, what I discovered is that when an organization gets to be of a certain size, the philosophies and values touted at the top of the organization may not be in line with the actions of the directors, supervisors, and staff members closer to the front lines of service. It took about eight months for me to see that most of what I thought was so great about my organization was actually a façade. The bad guys won here, too, just in different and less obvious ways.

This job was also the final straw regarding wages in the nonprofit sector. Even with a Master's degree I never made as much as $40,000 in annual salary. *Ever*. So, in November 2016 I started a virtual business with a network marketing skincare company to supplement my meager nonprofit earnings. I was trying to get ahead on my student loan payments.

I was stressed and questioning everything about my life and my career choices. When I'm stressed, I like to get a tattoo. The rush of adrenaline one experiences throughout hours of being stabbed by tiny needles can release a lot of negative energy. The week of my birthday in 2016 I booked an appointment with Jason at Electric Hand Tattoo Company in Nashville to have Nerdzilla emblazoned on my skin. I gave him full artistic control over the design. All I said was, "Nerdzilla" and he *nailed* it.

As significant as the Nerdzilla tattoo is, and as much as I love it, it was only the beginning of a list of new endeavors to come. In many ways, it marks the beginning of the metamorphosis of Kelly J. Mendenhall, BS, MPA, fancy-pants-intellectual into Kelly Nerdzilla Mendenhall, the girl who got her dreams back.

It gets worse before it gets better

In April 2017, I started to notice that I was having increased pain in my back and more frequent bouts of sciatica. I have lived with chronic aches and pains in my back and legs for most of my life. As a kid, I had horrific growing pains which I believe was due to growing so fast. In elementary school, my sister and I and had grown so quickly in such a short amount of time that the growth plates in our heels had actually fractured. *Yikes*, right? We had to wear super dorky looking rubber heel cups in our shoes for a long time. I never wanted to take my shoes off in front of my friends.

As a teen and young adult, I'd been in quite a few car accidents, including a roll-over wherein I was tossed around the inside of a Chevrolet Blazer several times. During my college years, I'd been struck on my driver's side by someone running a stop sign and got banged up pretty good in 2005; eight months later in 2006, I was rear-ended at a stoplight by some jackass playing with his radio. I really don't know how in the hell, outside of some small miracles and my dad serving as my guardian angel, I've gotten out of all of these things alive. Maybe there's no other reason beyond miracles and my dad, and maybe there doesn't need to be.

I digress.

By my senior year of undergrad, I was dealing with a lot of the ramifications of the accidents in the form of back pain, sciatica, memory loss, and other symptoms. Since then, I've always had some level of pain. I have lived with Ibuprofen, Aleve, and Tylenol on-hand at all times.

I started getting chiropractic adjustments in 2016 as my pain began to increase. My chiropractor did not mince words when he showed me my initial X-Rays. I was headed for spinal fusion surgery in the not-too-distant future if things didn't change and I didn't keep up with my adjustments. I listened and took him seriously, and it helped a lot. In April 2017, something changed, and the pain in my lower back and down throughout my left leg and foot was making it difficult to function every day. In early May I finally realized that this wasn't just a temporary flare, that something was seemingly *really* wrong, and saw my doctor. An MRI showed four bulging discs in my lumbar spine, all in a row. One of those discs had herniated and was compressing my spinal cord.

Additionally, one of my spinal discs appeared to be 90% gone, and I showed signs of moderate Degenerative Disc Disease throughout my spine. Osteoarthritis was also present in my lumbar spinal column. Over the next several weeks the condition of my left leg began to worsen, and new symptoms arose. My whole leg was constantly tingling now.

I saw a series of specialists who told me that I wasn't a good surgical candidate and needed physical therapy and pain management. They all seemed keen on prescribing me opioids, which I refused. I was regularly reporting that my pain was making me suicidal and I was feeling hopeless, and they would seem angry with me when I would turn down narcotics or become convinced that my pain couldn't be *that* bad if I weren't willing to accept the drugs.

Avoiding controlled substances and opioids was (and still is) a personal decision that I feel is right for me. With the history of addiction in my family, as well as my mental health history and addictive personality, I'm not willing to take the chance. I feared that I would be creating an entirely new problem for myself by inviting an opioid addiction into my life. Even though I was in a great deal of pain and was clearly *not* a drug-seeking patient, none of the specialists I saw during this period would complete paperwork giving me any time off of work to participate in prescribed aquatic physical therapy.

Finally, on June 20, 2017, I used my lunch break to see my primary care doctor. He could see the agony I was in, in spite of the copious amounts of nerve-blocking medications and muscle relaxers I was on. He filled out paperwork that day, and I carried it back to my office and submitted it to human resources. So, began my six-week medical leave.

Which turned into eight weeks.

And then 12 weeks.

Finally, after 16 weeks of being out on medical leave, I was still unable to return to work. I was officially "let go" from my position as Foster Parent Recruiter/Trainer on October 13, 2017; Friday the thirteenth.

Haven't found a way to kill me yet

My pain was mind-bending — a 10 out of 10 on the pain scale, 24/7, by July. I would often cry myself to sleep. When I was actually lucid, which wasn't often thanks to all the nerve blockers and other medication I was taking, I was a confused and miserable shell of myself. There was a period of months in 2017 that I don't have any recollection of at all.

My pain continued to get worse in spite of all of the medications, therapy, and repeated epidural spinal injections I received over the following several months. The scariest of symptoms included my entire left leg falling out from under me, limp and numb, at random times while I was walking.

When I was officially let go from my job, my human resources contact told me that it was time for me to fill out claim forms for long term disability. "Thank God," I thought. Because here's the real kick in the uterus — I *still* didn't have a firm diagnosis. I had started aquatic physical therapy in June and saw specialist after specialist from May to July. I went through the torture of three epidural spinal injections between June and October, but I was no closer to being any better by the time I lost my job.

So, of course, I thought the long-term disability policy was a God-send. The only form of steady income I had, had, between

June 2017 and October 2017 was from my virtual skincare business as well as a short-term disability policy that I carried with me from a previous employer. It was keeping my bills paid, but barely. And my income wasn't contributing anything to shared household expenses with my boyfriend, like groceries and utilities. The bulk of my financial support and physical care had fallen on the shoulders of my boyfriend.

Having the long-term disability benefits would provide a sense of security while I continued to fight with doctors and specialists, and against my own body, to get my life back. It turns out, though, that it wouldn't be that easy. My primary care doctor refused to communicate with the insurance company handling my claim. The specialists all failed to report the pain and other symptoms as I was reporting them. They would omit information in their clinical notes entirely or say that I was experiencing "moderate pain" when in actuality I had been in their exam rooms crying my eyes out, telling them that my pain was 10 out of 10 and begging for relief. They officially denied my claim for long term disability benefits in November 2017.

In addition to my physical health issues, I with Major Depressive Disorder (MDD), Generalized Anxiety Disorder (GAD), and Post Traumatic Stress Disorder (PTSD). My MDD and PTSD had been in remission for about four years. I didn't know it yet, but by December I was in the early stages of the worst relapse of my life. The symptoms peaked in February 2018, when I was hospitalized with Serotonin Syndrome.

My primary care doctor had convinced me, against my better judgment, to start taking a new anti-depressant, Cymbalta, in addition to Prozac, which I'd been on since I was 16. His motives were pure; he was concerned because I'd reported myself as feeling hopeless and having suicidal ideations because of the pain. Unfortunately, he was miseducated on both what Cymbalta could do for me and its interactions with Prozac.

He'd subsequently persuaded me (twice) to double the dosage of the Cymbalta. In February 2018 I was admitted to the hospital with severe heart palpitations, high blood pressure, blurred vision, hearing that sounded like I was underwater, and muscle spasms in my legs that were so severe you could see the movement in my muscles when glancing down at my legs. At times my muscles were so rigid and stuck in spasm that there would be visible lumps on my thighs.

I was released after one night of observation. The next morning, the doctor on duty accused me of having taken some synthetic marijuana or another street drug that could have made me so sick. I was *furious*. I also felt like hell because the nerve blockers and additional anti-depressant were addictive, and I'd now been without them for more than twelve hours.

The only way to reverse Serotonin Syndrome is to discontinue the medications that are causing it. The same doctor who accused me of taking recreational drugs advised me to taper down my medications. At that point, though, I was pissed off and didn't trust *anyone* outside of my pain interventionist. I was afraid that I would end up hospitalized again (or worse) and stopped taking everything cold turkey.

I went through three weeks of withdrawals. I mean, like, dopesick junkie withdrawals. I was hallucinating, having night terrors, and sweating bullets while also continually shivering. I couldn't eat for a week. I had diarrhea for days, and more than once thought I'd pass out on the toilet. It was and felt like I had been plunged into the depths of Hell.

I didn't think that my body could feel any worse than it had throughout the previous eight months, but I was *wrong*. Had I not been confident it would kill me to keep taking those meds, I probably would have given up getting off of them.

The business couch

Somehow - and believe me when I say that I don't entirely understand it myself - somewhere early in this journey (and through the fog of it all) I decided:

This was not going to be the end of my story. I was not going to give up that easily.

Fuck the doctors. Fuck the insurance company. Fuck the medications. I was going to make it through this if it killed me. Thus, the business couch was born. It became my hashtag and a lifestyle. I wasn't going to see myself as trapped and isolated from all the world's infinite possibilities. This was just another hurdle I had to get creative about climbing over.

If nothing else, I'm tenacious as *fuck*.

In March, after the fog of withdrawals lifted, I realized that for too long I had been betting on doctors to figure out what was wrong with me, employers to do the right thing, and insurance companies to honor their policies.

Worse than that though, was that throughout my entire adult life I'd bet on the sure thing, the safe bet. I thought that going to school, getting multiple degrees, and working my butt off would lead to a good life in which I would reap the financial reward and live a satisfying and productive life. None of that came to fruition. I was wasting time. And we don't have much time in this life to be wasting in the first place.

Between March and April of 2018, I had an epiphany: *I* was the thing I should be betting on because *I* was the only person who could climb out of the hole that I was in, physically, emotionally, and financially. No one else was going to save me; nobody else could. All of the so-called safe bets I'd made regarding my education and career path turned out to be things I thought I *should* be doing. They'd provided only a false sense of security and an assumption of entitlement for what I thought I *should* get because I had worked so hard.

The following is an excerpt from one of my blogs about my virtual business. I wrote it in the midst of realizing this epiphany, which turned out to be the only thing worth betting on in all of this, aside from betting on me.

> I have seen some posts floating around lately about how $500 a month could save homes from foreclosure, marriages from dissolving under the weight of financial stress, or provide families with a safety net and prevent them from going into debt over a surprise expense/catastrophe.
>
> That's why a lot of folks start virtual businesses.
>
> But what if a business could change your life? What if a business could save it, just by giving you a reason to get up and get going every day?
>
> I don't mean to sound melodramatic... stay with me.
>
> If you've read even a couple of my blogs, you'll know that I

talk about the shame-guilt-depression cycle that one goes through when dealing with chronic pain, and/or chronic illness.

We can't contribute as we should at work.

We lose our jobs.

We can't help out around the house.

We lose our disability.

We can't help pay for groceries or the roof over our head.

We can't; we can't, we can't.

'Can't' weighs on us and if we aren't careful, it can sink us like an anchor sitting on our chest.

But with this business, *I can.*

I *can* grow my audience, network, and customer base organically and honestly by maintaining consistency and employing a hell of a lot of creativity.

I *can* build my brand while lying flat on my back on the couch.

I *can* encourage and empower others and work every day with men and women who inspire and empower me.

I *can* study marketing statistics and strategies from my couch.

I *can* be answering questions and doing consultations via Facebook messenger while I sit in a doctor's waiting room for over an hour.
I *can* develop quality human relationships and communicate with my friends and business partners each day from wherever I am, physically and mentally. (And no one ever asks for me to give more than I can.)

> I *can* do all of this while helping others find more confidence, relief, and (maybe for the first time) love for the skin they're in. That is so effing *rad!*

That's the thing about Network Marketing that many folks don't talk about – it's *not* a pyramid scheme, there are legitimate companies helping change peoples' lives. People like me. That's why I decided to turn a mess into a message and tell anyone who would listen, my story.

We do not lose our value and worth because we lose control of our bodies. We live in a world with infinite possibilities, and there are ways to generate income from home in ways that didn't exist 10 or 20 years ago. A diagnosis doesn't have to be the end of a person's story. We are all the heroes of our own story, and *everyone* loves a hero.

What does it all mean?

As I write this (and for the foreseeable future), my health is my full-time job, and everything else is icing on the cake. It is now November 2018, and I have multiple diagnoses for things that are wrong with my neuromuscular system and spine. However, no one has nailed down the one thing that might be able to improve my quality of life significantly.

I have had three epidural spinal injections, one set of Sacroiliac Joint injections, three piriformis muscle injections, and two trigger-point localized cortisone shots into my ass. I've had two MRIs, one Electromyography (EMG) to test nerve conduction and functionality in my left leg and one Myelogram study. I have seen one orthopedic surgeon, two orthopedic neurosurgeons, two pain management specialists, one hip specialist, and one neurosurgeon's Physician's Assistant (PA.)

I participated in aquatic physical therapy and then standard physical therapy from June 2017 to March 2018. When my health insurance company stopped approving coverage for physical therapy, I took matters into my own hands and started going to water aerobics two to three days a week at the local Rec Center. I also tried walking regularly for cardio exercise because I'd put on 60lbs in my nine months spent entirely on the couch.

The trouble was, my muscles were so atrophied and depleted from my time on the couch that every time I'd walk around the block or get on a treadmill, my pelvis would shift due to having weakened stabilizer muscles. This would cause a domino effect that would throw my hips off, putting more pressure on my legs, knees, and feet, and then the nerve pain would ramp right back up to a 10. I'd be down for days at a time all over again.

I realized within a few weeks of this cycle that something had to change. I was going to have to start from the beginning to rebuild my body one piece at a time if I was going to get sustainable results. I decided to invest in a personal trainer. I mean, fuck, if I'm going to go into debt and rack up credit card bills it may as well be for something worthy, right? That's how I came to work with Jacob, my personal trainer at Muletown Rec.

May 3, 2018, was my first training session, and I've been seeing Jacob twice a week ever since, except for a couple of days where my back went out again. In general, most weeks, my care schedule is as follows:

Monday: Water aerobics, chiropractor
Tuesday: Workout with trainer
Wednesday: Cardio workout, maybe the elliptical
Thursday: Workout with trainer
Friday: Water aerobics

Each week I have at least one appointment with a specialist or doctor as well. I see my therapist 1-2 times monthly for trauma therapy and Eye movement desensitization and reprocessing (EMDR.) I see my psychiatrist once every six weeks or so. I see my pain management specialist at least once a month and my primary care doctor once every 3-6 months. I try to stick to an anti-inflammatory diet to keep the inflammation in my spine down. I take a laundry-list of supplements for inflammation as well. This shit isn't cheap, either.

After seeing the results of my Myelogram study, the neurosurgeon PA suggested that a dorsal column spinal cord stimulator implant would be the best way for me to regain quality of life and better manage my pain. My pain management specialist agreed with his assessment. I've decided to move forward with the implant, pending positive results from a week-long trial with an external device.

The thing is, I have several things that are just wrong enough to cause the pain and neuromuscular issues, but no singular thing that can easily be identified as the main culprit. That means I'm not a good surgical candidate. After a year and a half, I'm *still* fighting for my long-term disability benefits, a fight that appears headed to federal court.

Despite all the pain, heartache, and grief caused by doctors, specialists, and insurance company bureaucrats, I like to believe that life doesn't happen *to* us, it happens *for* us. I genuinely think that if I hadn't had a catastrophic physical health event occur, forcing me to stop everything I was doing, that I would have just kept trudging along only half-living my life until I died.

I would have kept plugging away in a career where my real value was never going to be recognized or adequately compensated. I would have stayed stuck in survival mode. I would have continued to push my true dreams farther and farther down inside of myself, eventually burying them underneath the kind of resentment that only comes from never realizing your true greatness.

Somehow, out of the biggest disaster of my life, I was reborn, and I reconnected with my most creative and determined self. In addition to the skincare business, I have a blog, *Nerdzilla Lives!* where I write about my experiences living with chronic pain and invisible illness while building a successful business from home. I started Nerdzilla Media so that I could accept freelance writing and editing work.

I was in a haze on the couch eating a peanut butter and jelly sandwich one night sometime in late 2017 when I suddenly declared, "I'm going to write a book! It's going to be called *The Stories My Tattoos Tell,* and it's going to tell my life story!" And, here we are. In December 2017, I connected with a fellow Network Marketing entrepreneur and now-recovering nonprofit professional like myself, Debbie Jo. Debbie Jo represents a different company, but we connected in a marketing mastermind Facebook group. We bonded almost immediately and became close friends who did a weekly Facebook Live series together on marketing and mindset. Within a few weeks, people started begging us to start a Podcast together, and so, *A Non Mom Happy Hour* was born.

Every week, Debbie Jo and I show up as authentically as we can and celebrate real ass, human women, whether they use their baby box or not. Our goal is to bring healing through laughter and community. We finally feel like we make the impact we always wanted to make and could never achieve in the nonprofit sector. Debbie Jo finds great joy in telling everyone that I'm going to be turning into a Cyborg soon and is begging the medical industry to create a mobile application that will control my stimulator implant so that she can say, "There's an app for that!"

Kelly Nerdzilla Mendenhall feels a hell of a lot more comfortable in her skin than Kelly J. Mendenhall, BS, MPA ever did. Every time I look down at my thigh and see Nerdzilla, a little movie plays in my mind, and I think of how far I've come from where I've been and where I have yet to go.

Resilience, tenacity, determination, and integrity.
These are the stories this tattoo tells.

Nerdzilla tattoo, designed and completed by Jason McDonald of Electric Hand Tattoo in 2016. Age at the time of completion, 34.

AFTERWORD

Things have a way of working out.

For those who may be curious about my relationships with family members who were mentioned in earlier chapters, I am delighted to report that my relationships with both my oldest sister and my niece have been mended. I'm very proud of my niece and who she has become as a person and adult, as well as a mother. My great-niece is a light in the world, she brings much joy to the family even from a distance.

My oldest sister and I reconciled around Thanksgiving of 2016. She thought she was sending a text to our other sister; somehow our phone numbers had become transposed in her iPhone address book. When we realized what had happened (after the initial shock wore off), she texted me to say that she didn't believe in accidents and that she missed me and would like to rebuild our relationship.

God works funny that way… It came as a total surprise, and I wasn't even sure at first that I wanted to go through the motions. It felt heavy and cumbersome to carry the weight of all of those feelings around, actively, again. My sister and I have both done a lot of growing, though, and a lot of healing from our own wounds and traumas. The people we are now are not the same people that fell out all those years ago.

As luck would have it, just over a year into my chronic pain and health catastrophe, my sister was diagnosed with Rheumatoid

Arthritis and Cluster Headaches. Due to my experience in self-advocacy and self-care, the grief and loss I endured over the person I used to be, and my experience with incompetent, asshole doctors, I've been able to help my sister a lot as she comes to terms with her new normal. I don't think that the timing was an accident.

Mechanendzilla

On December 14, 2018, I received my Boston Scientific temporary spinal cord stimulator implant. I embarked on a six-day trial to ensure that I would experience a significant enough change in my quality of life and pain management to justify moving forward with the permanent implant. There aren't many medical implants that a patient can "try out" before committing, so it's really pretty neat.

This device is designed to send electrical pulses to your spinal cord to overstimulate it and cut off pain signals from the affected body part(s) to the brain. Instead of feeling pain, you feel a sort of tingling sensation. If you have ever used a TENS unit for pain management and muscle rehabilitation, the feeling is very similar… except it's on the inside of your body.

The main difference between the temporary spinal cord stimulator implant and the permanent implant is that with the former, the electrical leads and battery pack are on the outside of your body, with small holes going into your spine from where the leads extrude. For this reason, the patient is at high risk of infection during the trial. I had to take antibiotics daily for the entirety of the trial and for a few days beyond.

I received my permanent implant on December 28, 2019. As I write this, I am four weeks and a few days post-op and doing well, aside from going a little bit crazy with cabin fever. I have 11 more days before I am allowed to bend, reach, stretch, and exercise as I did before. I am allowed to walk, but it took 3.5 weeks to be able to make a full trip through the grocery store without my incisions feeling as though they were being ripped open from the inside.

It will be about another year before I know what my quality of life will *really* be in the long-term with my implant. I must go through all seasons, temperature changes, resume my physical rehabilitation exercises and chiropractic care, and so on. As I lay here typing and reflecting, I can't help but feel incredibly fucking proud of myself.

I made it.

In spite of the evil doctors and in the face of financial poverty and professional ruin, I kept going. And I've begun building some really incredible things for myself. Where my baseline pain used to be a six or seven out of 10 on the pain scale, with 3 days a week with pain levels at 10 out of 10, my baseline is now one to three out of 10.

In the weeks since my permanent implant was placed, I have had 4 days of pain levels at a six or seven and only one day with pain at a 10 out of 10; that is a significant improvement. I remain hopeful that my pain will become even more manageable as time goes on. My brain essentially has to be retrained not to feel the pain in my leg and foot, and that will take some time.

My short-term health goals include being well enough once I am off restrictions to visit my family and friends in Michigan while my grandfather is still around. He turned 91 in December, and I fear and worry that I won't make it home in time to have one last quality visit with him. I'd also like to go out for a couple of book launch and reading events in different parts of the country in 2019. I'll be thankful for whatever progress my body makes and whatever my health allows.

In the meantime, I am *still* fighting for my long-term disability benefits from that insurance company full of motherfuckers and bastards (I'm sorry for the strong language, but sometimes it's necessary.) My lawyer is currently in negotiations with their attorney. I will be glad when I can put that particular worry behind me and stop swimming in a stew of financial anxiety and so that I may focus on getting better.

Whatever happens… well, at this point I know I can take it. I'm a lot stronger than I feel and a lot braver than I think. Thanks to one of the world's most competent trauma therapists, I'm learning to let go and surrender control, because I don't have any choice in the matter anyway.

And though I never, *ever* would have thought in a million years that I would become the person to say it – I have learned that it is all in God's timing, not mine.

This isn't the end of my story.

Something tells me it is only the beginning of the *really* juicy bits.

Please remember that none of the bad things that happen in

your life, none of the mistakes you make or hurts that you feel, have to be the end of Your story, either. We are all the heroes of our own story, and *everyone* loves a hero.

Mechanerdzilla illustration, created by Jason McDonalf in honor of my new beginning as a Cyborg.

AUTHOR BIO

Kelly Mendenhall is recovering nonprofit professional living in Middle Tennessee. A Southeast Michigan native, Kelly received her Bachelor's of Science and Master's in Public Administration from Eastern Michigan University, determined to change the world for the better by working in the nonprofit sector.

Kelly relocated to Nashville, Tennessee in 2013 in pursuit of life, liberty, and gainful employment. In 2017, Kelly became medically disabled and unable to work outside the home. It was then that she became reacquainted with her former, creative self, and dreamt again of becoming of a published writer.

Kelly is a Spoonie, author, Podcast co-host, entrepreneur, and self-care advocate living with chronic pain and invisible illness(es.) Her mission is to show the world that a medical diagnosis/diagnoses does not have to mark the end of one's story.

Kelly is freelance writer, a virtual entrepreneur in network marketing, and co-host of the podcast **A Non Mom Happy Hour.** Kelly is the ultimate dog mom to one Miss Rosebud Marie Eleanor Frances Mendenhall. She is cat mom to Pequeño, who she is pretty sure was touched by the angels. She's also the world's most proud Aunt and Great Aunt.

ACKNOWLEDGEMENTS

My Writing Coach and Mentor, Amber Jensen:
(**Author of** *This is Dirt*)

You had zero obligation to guide me through this process and yet were 100% dedicated to doing so. Thank you, from the bottom of my heart.

My Beta Readers:
Lorna & Olivia

You will never know what a service you provided me. You were my test audience, the way to prove to me that this wasn't a totally insane idea. And it worked out well. I thank you from the bottom of my heart.

Mike "Knappy" Heard

Friends for twenty-plus years and counting. I love you, dude, and I appreciate you so much for helping this book see the light of day. Can't wait to see you again on the other side of all of these years. Remember – this is not your final chapter or the end of your story. You are the hero of your own story and everyone loves a hero.

Copy Editor, my best friend, and my human panic room (thank you for that, by the way):
Cindil Redick-Ponte

Thank you for not hating it, and for even thinking it is pretty great. But mostly, thanks for not letting me look like an idiot. I love you, dude.

**My web designers, PR reps, and friends:
Claire Biggs and Jennie Armstrong**

I can't imagine having worked with anyone else. Thank you for being my two-woman Army. Can't wait to see what else we do together.

**Dr. Jay Schroder and Healthworks Chiropractic, Dr. John Welker (aka Dr. Unicorn,)
Dr. Glen Yank, and Kathy Keith, LPC:**

Each one of you have believed me and believed in me since the moment I first came into your care. I could never have asked for a better and more dedicated care team. This book wouldn't be possible if I was still curled up in the fetal position, crying in pain, or so depressed I couldn't bring myself to bathe or get out of bed, let alone write anything. Thank you all for being the kinds of healthcare professionals that actually care.

My personal trainer Jacob Chinander, and the staff and crew at Muletown Rec:

I am not a person who shies away from a fight — never have been. But I was losing the fight to get my body and my life back before you came along because I wasn't equipped with the tools I needed to rehabilitate and recover. I am forever grateful to you for all of the encouragement, training, guidance, and support. I am where I am because I found the right place and the right people for the job.

DEDICATIONS

To my mom,

Thank you for recognizing at a young age how important words were to me; how important reading and writing would always be. Not every parent would get their 8-year-old a typewriter for their birthday, no matter how much they begged. You did. You've supported and given me space for every single dream I've ever dreamt, and comforted me through every nightmare, literally and figuratively. I love you and I'm thankful I have you.

To my Dad, Jay Y. Mendenhall, R.I.P

You spent four years as my father on this Earth and have spent 32 years now as my Guardian Angel. You've done a hell of a fine job, then and now. I love you and miss you every single day and strive to always make you proud. I know in my heart you can see this.

My boyfriend and life partner, Nathan:

I know it's not always easy being in love with a dreamer or a bleeding-heart empath, and God knows I'm both. Thank you for taking such good care of us, of me, and for never questioning it for a second when I blurted out that day, over a peanut butter & jelly sandwich on the couch, "I'm going to write a book!"

To all of my nieces and nephews and great-nieces and nephews, by blood and by choice:

If you only ever learn one thing from me, let it be this: Nothing is worth putting your biggest shit-your-pants dreams on hold for. Well, ok, learn two things. Don't 'should' yourselves to death like I nearly did.

To every friend in every story of this book,

Thank you for making my life so much richer and more colorful. I love you guys. I hope I make you proud.

To every shit boss I've ever had and every petty bitch I've ever worked with,

Thanks for giving me every reason to never want to work for anyone else again. Y'all inspired some real shit to happen.